12/03

AMULET SONGS

AMULET

~ POEMS SELECTED AND NEW ~

SONGS

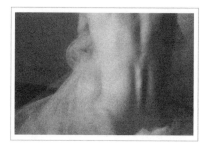

LUCILE ADLER

WITH AN INTRODUCTION BY V. B. PRICE

UNIVERSITY OF NEW MEXICO PRESS

ALBUQUERQUE

With special appreciation of my daughter,

Kathleen Harms, and Moriah Williams; and

for the ongoing affirmation of Barrett Price

who brought this book to life.

The Traveling Out and Other Poems
Originally published by MacMillan, 1960

The Society of Anna
Originally published by The Lightning Tree, Inc., 1974

The Ripening Light: Selected Poems 1977–1987
Originally published by Peregrine Smith Books, 1989

The Pink Madonna: Selected Poems
Originally published by Juniper Press, 1998

Printed by Sheridan Books, Inc.

Poems set in Sabon 10/14.5;
Display type set in Serlio and Frutiger

Design and composition by Robyn Mundy

©2003 by Lucile Adler
First edition
All rights reserved.

Library of Congress Cataloging-in-
Publication

Adler, Lucile.
Amulet songs : poems selected and new /
Lucile Adler.— 1st ed.
p.   cm. — (Mary Burritt Christiansen
poetry series)
ISBN 0-8263-3137-8 (alk. paper)
I. Title. II. Series.
PS3551.D6 A84 2003
811'.54—dc21
2003006263

9   8   7   6   5   4   3   2   1

MARY BURRITT CHRISTIANSEN POETRY SERIES

V. B. PRICE, SERIES EDITOR

Also available in the University of Mexico Press Mary Burritt Christiansen Poetry Series

Miracles of Sainted Earth
Victoria Edwards Tester

Mary Burritt
Christiansen
Poetry Series

Poets of the Non-Existent City
edited by Estelle Gershgoren Novak

CONTENTS

THE SOCIETY OF ANNA

THE RIPENING LIGHT

THE PINK MADONNA

INTRODUCTION

Lucile Adler is one of America's least known great poets. Nearing her eighty-first birthday, Adler has observed and chronicled the turmoil of the twentieth century in a way that reflects the circumstances of the life she chose to live far from the literary centers of our country in Santa Fe, New Mexico. Known to her friends as their most trustworthy confidant, to peace and social activists as a voice of calmness and courage, and to devoted readers as a candid, utterly straightforward writer of deep warmth and rational optimism, Lucile Adler and her work have become an "amulet," to quote the title of this volume, against the seductions of despair.

Adler moved with her family to Santa Fe from Cambridge, Massachusetts in 1950 as the Korean War darkened the nation. They lived on upper Canyon Road during the years that the state's rich, but eccentric, and largely marginalized literary history was taking another turn with a newer group of exiles from the mainstream. The poet and translator of Lao Tzu, Witter Bynner, had led the way, living in Santa Fe since 1922. Robinson and Una Jeffers had come and gone visiting Freda Lawrence in Taos in the 1930s. D.H. Lawrence had left in 1925 but his aura lingered. The great New England poet and critic Winfield Townley Scott was to arrive in 1953. Frank

Waters, Paul Horgan, Fray Angélico Chávez and Sabine Ulibarri were still hard at work. Georgia O'Keeffe was still headquartered and working up river in Abiquiu. And photographer Eliot Porter was soon to move to New Mexico. Lucile Adler, herself, a young mother of two, wouldn't publish her first book of poems until seventeen years after she and her husband had settled in Santa Fe.

Adler belongs to a generation of New Mexico writers and artists who saw the state emerge from WW II not only as the secret capital of America's Cold War nuclear weapons research, but also as an aesthetic enclave of writers, musicians, and artists who continued New Mexico's long history of being the hideout for creative people who wanted to work in a uniquely southwest American context while maintaining ties with a wider audience.

Tending her family, Lu Adler stayed, as she told me, by the kitchen window looking out on the world. Even though her poems appeared in *The New Yorker, The Nation, Poetry Northwest*, and a score of other major magazines, only those who love poetry, and are familiar with New Mexico's creative life, are likely to know much about her. And yet, she is virtually lionized by other poets around the nation.

May Sarton wrote about one of Adler's later books *The Pink Madonna*: "Lucile Adler gives us poems as hermetic and open as Georgia O'Keeffe's landscapes that haunt for the same reason, plain and mysterious, rich in their austerities. . . . [She] is a poet on her way, to be met and recognized again with joy as she travels out, this time farther into the lives of women."

James Merrill wrote that "Lucile Adler's region is not so much the Southwest as the heartland common to us all. Her sane, vivid poems are among its natural wonders."

Demetria Martínez observed that "great poetry draws attention to that which is greater than itself, testifying on

2

behalf of our propensity for love, justice, or their opposites. Adler offers such a testimony."

Publishers Weekly wrote of her 1974 book *Society of Anna*,

> Relying heavily on the landscape of the American South-west for their narrative context and fecund imagery, these fine poems reflect a struggle to perceive the world realistically, without sacrificing either compassion or hopefulness. Adler wishes to focus on that which transcends the ordinary ('a radiant spirit on the road alone/among many, shining out to sustain you') as symbolizing justice—to her mind, a more honest idea than redemption in a world such as ours. . . . Despite Adler's attention to the difficult or the painful, her insistent sense of fairness ('After all, I only want to say: Wrong's wrong') allows her to bypass the maudlin and sentimental.

Perhaps Winfield Scott said it best when he reviewed her first book, *The Traveling Out*, published in 1967 by Macmillan: "An exceptionally distinguished first book by a woman who becomes at once one of the really interesting poets in America. The book is filled with intuitive wisdom, a strong feminine objectivity, and I like the way in which it cries 'Risk Joy.' The combination of substance and the grace of language makes it a poetry of remarkable beauty."

Lucile Adler long ago chose what she considered a full life—a life of love and family, of steady writing, of political commitment and quiet, tireless work for human rights. Her knowledge of how lives are led and suffered, her passionate concern about the fate of all the people and children of the world, her loving eye and dedicated curiosity, give her poems a universal kindness and vivid sympathy so startling and uncommon in their beauty and metaphor that you can say with surety that no one has read the likes of them before.

And while her personal life has been withdrawn and even stoic in her attentiveness to what is, in all its beauty and all its contradiction and misery, personal hardship and tragedy have given her work an unwavering strength, a spine that simply won't buckle. Her sister, who suffered from polio, spent her life in an iron lung. Her husband, Nat Adler, was a pilot in WW II who was shot down over Germany and spent years in a Nazi prisoner-of-war camp, the same camp, in fact, where a month before his capture, the "great escape," memorialized in the film starring Steve McQueen, was staged. After her husband's premature death in the early 1980s, Adler's years of disciplined poetic work took form in a number of books dedicated "in memory of Nat."

Though Adler has not published as extensively as some professional academic poets, her poetic output is enormous and she has written virtually every day of her adult life, and continues to do so, producing poems at a prodigious pace. The poems in the final selection of this volume, entitled "Age Without Medals," were written after a near fatal illness left Adler so weakened she was no longer able to live by herself. A number of these poems are the result of her daily writing practice carried out in a nursing home.

The last poem of this selection is entitled "With Certainty and Praise." It begins,

Here are the hours of defeat
To memorize
and pass along, long days
to tear apart, fold open
and write notes on notes
Complaining about all
The losses. . . .Tonight, when all the doors

Should stand open and
all the light should
stream through,
And what is learned
Erase itself down
To the frayed white page,
The long day memorized,
Ready to be passed on,
And graded at last,
With certainty and praise. . . .

Here is Lu Adler still attentive as ever to the way life actually is, never for a moment judging it wanting, never for a moment denying its excruciating confusions, loving what is, as it is, as hard as it may be. People younger than Lu, like myself, who've been befriended by her, sense, sometimes, that's how she's lived the life that was hers to struggle with, quietly and without medals, risking joy, has been, and remains, a model for what it means to be mature.

In a collection of prose poems entitled "Letters to the Young," Adler wrote about the Plain of Jars, where numerous battles were fought in north-central Laos in the early 1970s during the Viet Nam War:

Do you remember when two of the Delgado boys. . . had the mumps—their necks swollen into their round faces were grotesque—and they went running about in the field near the house? What a commotion! Worse than the day George fell out of the poplar tree. Mother had to be revived too—unable to face the idea of death—George's, yours, others in places like the Plain of Jars later.

Don't be frightened. Though later you may not trust love or even the field of gramma grass or the street shaking under your feet; though nothing will be secure or simple for a time, you will try (I hope you will try) to find trust like a kernel of live wheat in the field where the boys with mumps, playing, trampled down the wild grasses. You may even find love.

Remember how the wind, rising, used to shake the dry sunflowers under the Russian olive trees? Then we would go in for supper. Now the world is crowded with men like broken pieces of glass, and we have allowed hatred, jagged glances, a brutal reality to pierce us. We fight it as we do our poor enemies jabbing into the Plain of Jars. . . .

So much fever has poured out that everything is changed; the field, the poplar trees, the mud gold after rain tracked into the house, have other names, perhaps can't exist much longer. (You were reading *The Wind in the Willows* that fall, while I read Rimbaud's *Season in Hell*.). . . .

Trust will come back, if it will, like the new rice in the Plain of Jars, the green harvest, magic grains of rice or wheat that could revive the field where you and the Delgado boys wrestled. (We don't *know* this can happen, but it must be planned for, in case, as though—all the way to the world's end if necessary.). . . You have no choice, really, but to try. And remember, as you search emptiness stubbornly for fidelity and love, remember how stubbornly people lean on their simple lists. That is where we begin; it is the least we can dare. You will find your own vivid paths and ways, but remember, even Rimbaud cried out at the last, 'Let us never curse life.'

Lu Adler often writes to the younger part of us and, perhaps, of herself, that part of us that believes the truth is what is said of it, who can't imagine that anything could be so horrible as reality has turned out to be, who is as surprised to find itself growing old and strange as it is shocked that history has taken the turns that it has—the turns that are by now so familiar and so redundant that no one can believe that the fates, with all their pride of craftsmanship, would let them happen again so soon. She writes from both the perspective of an adult who has not forgotten what it means to be a child, and the perspective of an observer who is steady, clear, fearless, and still deeply given to this life despite its profusion of sorrow.

It's telling that Lucile Adler chose to associate this largest selection of her life's work with amulets, and the poems themselves with the charms and incantations on amulets that are meant to protect their wearers against evil or to aid them in fulfilling their lives. Privately, and perhaps selfishly, I find the publication of these "amulet songs," all in one place and in substantial numbers, to be a deep and uncanny source of strength and reassurance much like the bestowal of a charm might be, one that, indeed, transforms us so we remember that hope is never to be forgotten as the single most practical force we have against the futility of despair and the jaggedness that pierces and bloodies our world.

V. B. Price
Albuquerque, February 2003

THE TRAVELING OUT

The Traveling Out

I wonder, since we are both traveling out,
If we may go together? Thank you.
You may be sure you will be alone
And private as though I were no one;
God knows, I do not wish to increase your burden.
Naturally these airports, these blinding cities
And foundry lights confuse you, make you
More solitary than the sight of one lost lamp
Across a bare land promising life there,
Someone over that field alone and perhaps
Waiting for you. That used to be the way.

Feel perfectly free to choose how
You will be alone, since we are going together.
Of course, I never move, I merely hold you
In my mind like a prayer. You are my way
Of praying, and I have chosen you out of hordes
Of travelers to speak to silently, on my own.
I will be with you, with your baffled anger
Among fuming cities, with your grief

At having lost dark fields and lamplight.
It is my way of moving, of praying:—

Oh, not to give you someone like me,
That's all over, impossible, I go nowhere;
And besides nothing is given, absolutely nothing
And no one, only white sermons among
The white of a billions bulbs. No,
Sitting here behind my shutters at twilight
I am stretching over the blazing lanes,

The dazed crowds jostled and razed
By light, only to join your mind and guide you
Gently; leading you, not, alas, to my own lamp across
The fields of the world, nor to a cosy last
Prayer of lamplight blessing the fields of the air
But out into hordes of stars that move away
As we move, and for which your traveling
Prepares you to go out a little more boldly,
All alone as I am alone.

Country School

First, children, you may smell the fires
In the fields outside where kernels of corn shine
And the gnarled apples are drying.
That will be our morning prayer.

Now, to what will you pledge allegiance?
To this poor village where the lean cattle
Graze under a sky the color of husks?
To this schoolroom full of cracks for autumn to enter?

(We can never be too open.)
To mountains that are roots?
To harvests of clouds? To cities?
To futures beyond the mountains? Manuel?
You pledge allegiance to Rosa and Toni?
Very well. That will do.

Here is the test for today:
    What is a harbinger?
    What is flight?
    Of what types of flight

Is man capable?
Decline the verb "to be."
What is consciousness?
(We will expand upon this later.)
What is the meaning of apples
Brocading an unsound tree?
Read from the script of birds.
Rosa, when the bony horses are brought
To the corral and the wind sharpens over the mountains,

What is coming? Cold nights on a mat near
    the rafters of your house?
Simplify.   Winter is coming.

Over the rocks the clouds fly;
As over the fact flies the meaning.
Remember this when you fondle seed for the hard fields
Or taste cider from an apple a wasp bit, or
When you run, holding hands or knives
By the knife-strong streams of snow.
Anna, be quiet. Contemplation
Is not only for sixth-graders.

The door has blown open; cold and the corn shocks
Border our narrow desks. Go home through them slowly,
Attend the fires in the fields, concentrate,
School is out. Tonight study the products of Georgia
And your multiplication tables through ten.
Tomorrow again, Discipline.

Certainties

What she suspects the others seem to know:
How motives solid as the flesh of birds
Shift in a shifty wind and dip
To the ground they all must find.
Everything changes as they stand
Watching the birds, pondering their own
Wings and capacity for flight:

What they know, below their feathered words,
Is how words stand for things that dip
And swing above crevasses in the mind;
They suspect, therefore, there is no ground—
As she begins to grow wings in the bone
To own a vantage others disavow,
And shift suspicion into certain flight
That dips between a snowy sky and snow.

Long Ago

Long ago, little one, a white horse
Grazed on a willow plain
As you rode by asking about death.

Under a milky sky braided with light
The horse leaned over the green furze
That lighted the long red earth;

On that day when hawks trailed
Ribbons of cloud over the sky,
No one could lie to you.

"You will be ribboned with clouds,
You will be water and willow
For a shining horse alone

On a long red plain; you will be wind
Like silk in the mane of the white horse."
For who could lie to you, riding

So sleepily by the willows
Where water gleamed in white pools
On the red soil, holding a wide sky.

Do you remember, long ago,
As the horse flashed by,
How uncompromising we were about death?

Then we braided your pale hair
And let you sleep the rest of the way.

Portrait with Lemon Leaves

Paint us at home in umber rooms,
Our hands folded over the snowy cloth
Or stroking a child's chrysanthemum head
Near loaves of bread and lemon leaves:

Let our faces be drawn with love,
Hollowed by kisses as mottled stone
Is hallowed by feet passing in
To see something true:

Let our hair, caught by scraps
Of jay blue ribbon, flaunt brightness
When we lean under lamplight true
As homes lit by those who risk love:

If you must lie, let our bones bit
By toil glow tenderly over a shaggy child
Stealing smooth fruit from a bowl;
Let your brush light us, render

The sagging flesh creamy and bronze;
And let us emerge alive, limned with light
As love is; each of us a masterpiece

Glistening from your hands, but authentic,
True as we all are true.

Desert Almanach

How well-connected God is in the land!
His great rock-ribbed relations stand
Avuncular and lava-browed; storm ties
Striping their weathered breasts; rocky
Streams bounding with their brown blood.
Nobility frowns on their right hand.

Eagles crest their vast armoires where bones
Of mutinous small birds are pressed;
Under giant claw-feet, wings like lancets
And manes of common beasts fret the sand.

Stony aunts with amber crosses and insects
On their breasts are claques calling
Him Nephew; they dream how dignity
Once frolicked in coronets of green leaves
Over the bright indentured sands;

Erect now, the color of port, they stand
Quaffing snow from baronial mantels and

Exhorting their scion's presence in the land.
While He, distracted from a flower in His mind,
Frowns and moodily flings down lightings
And His orb of sun, unimpressed by clamant ties
Or genealogies of stone.

The Lonely Neighbor

I know you though you go alone
To dine on rinds of love and sorrow
From a round plate like a stone.

I know your face, your flat disdain
At being you instead of star
Alone with hunger on the shore;

I do not mean to stroll your pain
Nor patronize the bare mind
Shining, waiting for a loaf of light;

I am the guest who sits to share
The napkin draped about the stone
That hides your hunger from his own,

A neighbor placed on the white shore
To taste this sorrow and this light
And, uninvited, ask for more.

Celebration

We have our choice today
Among the plantations of light
And luminous woods
Where blackbirds sparkle.

We may go into any landscape
For all the light is fertile
And awaits our coming:

Though we are peons we may choose to bear light,
To celebrate gravely, to hold our heads high
Under our shady hats with their bright streamers.

A Treaty of Liberation

Where to negotiate?
Not here, the pines on guard
Are black, their loyalty not assured.

We must talk unheard
By so much as a mountain lion
Or suave bird:

Perhaps in an old church
Leaking young roses?
I understand your reluctance;

Some monsignors suppress
Their springs and favor stones;
Too high a price for silence.

No, we can't communicate
From the carved dark close
Of a saint's soul,

Nor base concessions
On a mountain lion's growl.
But there is a desert

Deserted by Zouaves and oil
Where hard mercenary winds
(Which alone can't be trusted)

Will bind us paw to paw
Until we drive soft bargains
And make boundless

The boundaries of mind
Through blue ententes of space;
Then radical roses will spring

To speak wild treaties,
And our alliance will rise
Wide among black pines

And birds like flags
From stone, rising,
And men rising, revived
And sovereign.

In Memory of Certain Sapphire Flowers

Let the weak be merciful.

Let them scavenge from the rubble
Of Wisdom a scrap of wisdom to wave
As they ragtag to the barricades,

Where in shattered layers of the past
The fossil flowers grow. There
Let them pluck the absolute color

Of tenderness, last shown in the lives
Of old sages, whose cries of warning
Leaked through history to carve

A memory of wise men lost, and
Certain sapphire flowers saved in stone.
Let the weak raise on their banners

Those invincible flowers, and salute
The old brave men as they charge,
But mildly, blue fields folding over steel—

And charge again in ranks of tenderness:
Lest rotted stem and flame they yield,
And the hard past be acted out again

And the wrong barricades be won:
Let the weak be merciful.
Pray: Let the weak grow strong.

27

A Wedding Near Pilar

Among these lava rocks, a wedding.
The bride wears peach flowers
And a hawk circles the running water.

No one knows what is best:
Is it right to carry lighted candles
Before dark across the water?

Or right to break off peach flowers
For a crown, however humble? The hawk
Shadows the rocks with foreboding.

Is it the right season?
Will the bride remain faithful?
The hawk depends on abundant waters

Near the black-clad guests;
The bride will depend—on what?
Does she know what will nourish her,

What is best? Here is a wedding, a spray
Of peach, a jet of water upon rock,
Even a ceremony of wings;

As they light the candles they wait
For the sure-footed groom to step over,
But no one is sure of him,

Or if the wedding should go on
Beside the running water,
Or if it is all for the best.

In the Parish of Christo Rey

All the dark women common as twine
Rise on the night road bearing candles;
Wrapped in black shawls they wind
Past bonfires and the dying fruit trees
Whose branches are black baskets among stars.

As the dark women walk the winding road
Shielding their candles with thin hands
And bending their hidden faces, the night wind
Begins to stir. Slowly they move now,
Hiding in a bent frieze their old hunger

For birth, for daughters to star the rough bark
Of the fruit trees shawled in night.
The women pause, cupping their secret light;
As the night wind fills its basket of branches,
Their candles bloom on the night road
Like constellations waiting to be born.

After Van Gogh

Who can go undaunted
Between the giant sunflower sun
And phlox-white oily whorls
Of heat that blind? Between
Roiled blue grains
Of mountains
And grinding flowers of light?

Who can go on,
Frail as a black cosmos seed
Or hot pollen flake
Of yellow sand exploding

Through turmoil
Of white, of yellow fire
Coiling mountain
And man-form
Into one blind storm
Of cornflower and bone dust:

Who can go undaunted
Towards the far well
And the cold cup
Beaded with reason,
And not be lost?

Whisper for a Daughter

Birdling, be honest.
Say only so much, if more light
Cannot be imagined.

Promise only that which will be;
As, the wind rising,
Trees rising, white waves.

Use a willow whistle
Or be silent if truth interferes
With a salt-bright word.

Sometimes pluck feathers
From the talk of others
To weave into your silence.

Build, little bird,
From your frosty chores
A white perch of candor.

One day, the heart that nests
In your mouth will fly
Out; it will have straight wings,

And it will honor all the silences
Rising to meet it.

As in Tibet

What is happening? What is happening?
In the hill towns the snow is falling
And in Tibet the bells are capped by snow.
Here and there wild ponies run over stones.

A million women kindle fires and lay cloths
For men they love or hate
In clapboard houses or mud houses at twilight.

The mist in the valley is rising.
A great man is out looking for great men.
Someone is stabbing his brother.

A little girl lifts a gray cat with a cat's grace
Into a room out of the falling snow.
What is happening?

They are carving rafters, carving decisions.
A woman with braids changes her love
From one man to another.

Hunters in a remote place climb
Through the mist to caves and ringing bells.
Stews are bubbling; a gaunt face prays angrily.

The nations, in anguish, ban death at frontiers
Where ponies plunge thigh-deep in snow:
And all the children offer bowls of milk to gray cats.

In a hill town a man and a girl walk,
Enduring, as in Tibet, the hungry hours till night
And then engaging night.

Anita with White Lilacs

Anita, before you go home
Under the parchment sky livid
With white and brown stains of thunder,
Put down your lilacs, sit with me
On this creamy-lichened stone awhile;
Now. Nothing is pure white,
Not even those clouds swollen
With whiteness we use to lure you upwards.

The light dust of the road binds your toes
And rises onto the lilacs with their brown stems.
Nothing is pure white, Anita, not linen,
Nor Irish lace, not lilac nor altitude.
Wait here awhile.

Needles of sun embroider noon,
And sweat smocks your gauzy dress
As I admire your dry brown hands
And agate eyes appraising
The clouds that warn you home. Wait a bit:

Passion is always noon, a degree of whiteness
Scrawled through the dark bronze thunder.
You are silent as a brown moth
Tossed in the sun, lost in flecks of light—

If you will stay, Anita, we will place
The wiry stems by your feet in cool water.
Then I will lie to you; cool drop by drop
I will lie, assuaging your thirst

With the damp smell of tales I will guarantee,
And scrolls drawn from the gleaming dust
Of summer mountains steaming with snow.

Anita, rest awhile.
Dig your shy toes in the amber stream bed
Where I will force threads of water
And that coolness I promised.

Then at least I will revive:

While you start home holding white lilacs
In your mothlike hands, trickles
Of water and sun staining you as you go
Slow through your own storm of wonder
At the hot and toppling heart of noon.

For Fanny Lou Hamer

Wise men
Call you a great event
That, slow as a seed
Opening
Blasts the resentful clay
To grave
And purposeful flowering;

An event,
An idea in the dark
Waiting
Brave and colorless
As sun
To announce, as sun does
The shocking plain
Truth of day,
What is true and plain:

Waiting,
You may scorn

Blessings
On your hardy "yes"
That needs only light
To flower;
Scorn history
Trumpeting
After the event,
And honors
Common as our clay
In which you wait,

Sad and triumphant,
For death or welcome,
For death and welcome;

But you are a bright act in the land.

A morning glory opens where you stand.

Good Night

To all that is alive, good night.
To all who walk in the cold
Knowing their own features,
And to all who go, silent, past
Lamplight not knowing how to share
What is known of the cold
Or of craving and loving:
To loneliness itself, shuddering alive
Outside at night; to the cold,
The livid or calm cold
Thriving over weak men who dare
Dream love beside a fire
And amber hives and honeyed days—
Dreams sleep alone. Nor does cold
Care. But for all creatures
Bearing night, unloved and lost,
For all alone learning to be alone
Past love, who still endure the cold,
A knowing spreads and grows—
The drop of dawn we crave and share.

We Are All Walking the Same Road

I

We are all living at once and walking the same
road on the same cold afternoon. Blue cities shine
in the distance tender as misted grapes, full of lives
tapered and warm as Malagas. The cities are here, and
their lives, mixed with our own harvests, join the walk
home from our blue fields held in by mountains.

II

It is no one's fault that when we reach home we cannot
prevent the cold nor grasp the flames of the great minds.
We dream of them by the hearth in our house on Abeyta,
knowing we all live at once.

III

A great mind? A whole populace in the skull of one man,
working together to construct an Attica solid as sky and
crisp as snow, impervious to Time. The minor great burn
with other fires which we must sort as we do the wools
dyed by pomegranate from those that drank cochineal.

IV

Our homes shine among dark leaves under the mountains.
Tendrils of damp hair, of lives, bend as hunger is served
before the fire . . . for greatness itself or for its
semblances. Prices are juggled, expeditions planned,
wines judged and diluted with snow; someone laughs, and
an old aunt whines for a bunch of grapes before she dies.
She can see them in the blue fire.

V

In our houses life grows like cities with many towers,
like shaking mountains of flame on the hearth, like
piñons slowly. There is nothing to mourn, so long as
each fire is fed, each house faces outward, and each
sleeper under his dyed rug feels the snow of far places
on his face.

VI

Genius though hidden is shared, a secret brandy warming
the throats and veins of strangers. The genius of a time
is the amplitude of humble men who hold such liquor well,
and from a tangled memory of stars and sextants, blue
grapes and seas, blued steel and gaseous silk sails
make marvelous maps showing Abeyta Street vaster than Asia.

VII

Deep below the Barrier reef, at the heart of the dark
pomegranate seed or the crystal, Man walks, we all walk,

molecules in a space that is no longer blue, but familiar
now as lead or sapphire, while the genes grow on a vine
of life that is known. Even we . . .

VIII

It will be tomorrow soon. Time to go out. The wings
of Mercury are folded inside our sleepy heads. Now the
children laugh, are scolded and stuffed by an old aunt
with sugared bread, prepared . . . There is need for
passionate haste, for those wings to open, for morality,
fresh latitudes . . .

IX

We are living all at once, walking on Abeyta road
past blue cities and harvests of understanding. Child,
dear neighbor, love, what is it we are sharing, sheer
as the form of our fire last night and related to the
sun whose common dye lights all our faces? There is
no genius in the face of the genius that makes us walk
here, alone of course, but hand in greater hand.

THE SOCIETY OF ANNA

An Obscure Way and a Clearing

If I learn for sure
I am not sure
I will tell you the way.

After all, if I arrive
I will arrive
By my own route;

If I find a path
It will be a path
Through my own storm:

Would you endure
My saying "endure"
The storm that broods over

Your path; your truth
Shaken as truth
Is by a dark wind?

I weave out and in.
What is out I take in
To sort and chart;

How can you blame
Me, when I blame
My own way and heart?

If I find a clearing
Should it be your clearing,
Too, marked by a clear sign?

If I were sure
I might risk a sure
Gesture, a paper map held out

Showing a certain way
That could not blow away
If we set our hearts on it like rocks.

At the Cave Mouth

Fires
Amber as eyes watching
Pine boughs burn
Lie down on the cave floor

A woman with oiled hair
A gentlewoman wrapped
In bloody hides and red fox fur
Stirs embers with a bone

Then opens her cloak to share
Nakedness
In the stone-cold dark
The first civility

Overhead
Painted gods
Hidden by night-smoke
Chase a red antelope

The woman blouses a child
At her bare breast
And enfolds a worn hunter
Glistening

Dreams

Oxblood polish on earth
Floors, flourish of horns
Through arches of rare wood
Where dyed flowers on wool

Hang at cold openings
Inventions   Civilities
Even love
Later

The fire lies down
And dies in the dark

Overhead
Warrior gods
Loose red spears and sleep
Unseen
Man and child
Swathed in silence
Sleep

At the cave mouth
Wakeful
Soul leaping white dawns
The woman chases
Tomorrow   alone

From the cave mouth
The sparks of her eyes
Look out

"The Heart Determines"
                    —*Martin Buber*

Five white stones in an earthen bowl
Or five men in a stone valley
Between mountains; or any number.

Who will examine them?
Who will study the water,
The women, the hands
That make them shine sleekly?

Who will prove the men are not stones,
Streaked by darkness as men are?

Who will prove the stones are not men
With dark eyes, lolling in streams
Where live women wade?

Meanings run through our hands
And over the stones like water:

Who will determine,
Who will explore and determine
What is worth stroking and loving,

What sums we must guess to make one?

The mountains don't care.
No valley or clay bowl holding men
Or stones loosely, cares or will care.

One man willing to take stones
Or lives in his hand, five or one,
Bends over water, kneels
To drink meaning

That tastes like a woman wading a stream.
Will he marry? Let him prove love.

In the end his whole heart will determine.

Geranium Flame

Anna runs home under a dark beam of air coming near.

We go home too along the ashen road to meet
Closed fists or open arms; fearful or unafraid
Go to prepare red wine, bread on a red cloth,

Ample portions of heartbreak or honey
Under eaves waiting to bear the weight coming near.
What oppresses, oppresses us all.

Faces linen with fear, we light brass lamps
Or marigolds in a jar, or like Anna, love:
Bravura alone can never tend house here.

All we own—yellow kerchiefs of light—we give
At doors compassion opens on charred night.
All we are, meager or brave, we kindle and prepare

As thunder crashes on lamplight. Anna, stranger,
Dear friend, defiant gifts gather and rise, sparks
Tremble into bloom on the hearth that shares us.

What oppresses, oppresses us all—
Each rare geranium of flame rising alone
To light the way past fear or follow

Though the dangerous dark has fallen and is here.

53

The Twelve Dancing Princesses

You were old yesterday.
After the Twelve Dancing Princesses
   you read Kafka.
Mother burned homemade bread
   and fed you anger.
Father was excitable.
In no time you ran from the meadow
   full of yarrow
Into the resinous woods.

You kicked your heels in the pine cones
   and told Mother No
When she called. Then you lay down
   on the pine needles,
Excitable and angry—surrounded by wild lupine
   and a tribe of wandering boys . . .

Later you told the other princesses
   how queenly queens are

And you told them, not how lonely it is
    in the pine woods,
But how exciting. Secretly you cried a little
    behind a hand stained with resin.

For a while yet you tried to dance
    in the yarrow and mullein
But your laughter was shrill.
Around you, crazy tribes, encircling trees.
Mother had nothing to say but *Midnight.*
    Midnight . . .
Father, excitable, said come home.

No one gave you work shoes, a brown map, a knapsack,
    or geography lesson
Before you set out, scared, to explore
    more woods and perils.

An old woman picking nuts like a squirrel
    passed by:
All you princesses will have to make do
    without magic, she said.
She did not offer a nut with a dress in it
    beautiful as the sun.
She did not offer burned bread or a book
    by Kafka.
She looked and looked at you.
In spite of what the queen and your excitable father
    fear,

You are a hard worker and virtuous,
    I can see that, she said.
As for love—you can make potions
    as well as anyone.
Then she went away in the woods.

Of course you tried for a long time to break
    open her words
For their kernel. The dancing princesses
    waited for
Someone to tell fairy tales, or an old woman
    to step
Into their charmed circle with charms, perhaps
    a vial
Of joy found in dark woods among mushrooms.

Now you look at your sisters,
    your ancestors.
Your silence says in spite of everything
    you will go far.
Princesses, you will have to go so far
    and then farther.
You step into the yarrow field
    and hold out your arms.

Something winks in the woods.

We were all old yesterday.

Impatience Is a Flower

Anna plants a red impatiens in the sand.
Last night a pack of dogs howled in the hills;
A child, fed codeine, cried and slept a while;
A pride of planes passed on a screen to war—

Today their shadows strike her as she stands
On ground alive with ants along a trail;
Their morning wings roar in her morning mind;
She lifts her trowel and prepares to kill.

Last night she told her lover love was dead,
Flicked off their leaf-green blanket
And alone in bed, cried like a fevered child.
Her trowel flashes to destroy the trail.

Loaded with pride, far planes dive down to fire.
She meant to tend her world with gentle hands,
But war inside denies man, child and sandy root—
A crying grows. Dogs bark in the far hills:

A rash of fires hides the distant ground.
There is no codeine for the pain she knows
When wings streak low to drive her garden wild,
And war's impatience kills what Anna grows.

Weather Before Women

weather
changes
before women

legions
of leafy warriors
green warring trees caught in storm
and princesses in pointed doors
pierce us like fire

old winds mount
young winds mounting
green blood
lost austerities young once
signal
fire storm weather

no leather or lead shield
worn inside or tree bark
guards

burned throats
where green birds hide
and women
changed
stretch pointed wings
in their own time
over storm
all stormy leafy women must pass through

Dark by Dark Is Taken

Gold in the trees
Honey on the floor
Who believes in giving?
Who knocks at the door?

Everything is taken
The neighbor asks for more
Honey for his lips
A mattress on the floor

Night is coming closer
Gold is shaken loose
Agonies unspoken
Force her to her knees

Where is kindness, neighbor?
Here's a broken jar
Night is coming closer
Gold bleeds from the trees

Only dark is left
To fall on and adore
Dark by dark lies shaken
Mattressed on the floor

What rage brings you, neighbor?
Everything is taken
Night is coming closer
With another suitor

Frantic at the door
Who believes in giving?
Dark by dark is taken
Who loves anymore?

After the Garden

After we left the garden
We found
Orioles in the forest
And yellow apples harmless
As orioles on sunny days

Sometimes
We made fires to roast apples
Made wheels painted sumac and gold
Sometimes
Rushed apples and orioles
    to mud palaces where
Splashed with sun on sunny days
We even made love

After
Our children grew towers
From stolen black seeds
We were homeless
But sometimes

Yellow orioles flashed signals
Through forests of cities they made

Sometimes
On sunny days we market again
For yellow apples
And sometimes find

A garden laughing in dark eaves

When the People Are Avenues

There are days when the people are beautiful
And recognize one another on a street
Bordered with yellow flowers, burning leaves
And the clarity of an enduring sky.

On these days, even the evil man
With his fervent eyes is understood,
And tranquility is a passion.

Then squashes and melons are solid
Unger the crisp fingers of housewives
Who know one another, who gaze
Far down the burnished avenue
Which never ends, but is seen only
In moments of laughter, ease and profundity;

A day of recognition,
Of perfect motion and comprehension,
Of knowledge sound as melons
Or sure as the waking fingers of women
On a plain day glazed with sunlight

When the people are beautiful,
Are avenues bordered with yellow flowers
And burning with recognition.

Flight #

No, I'm not ready; though I've packed and sorted
And wrapped and packed again, not ready at all.
I don't know if my suitcase is empty or full—
Can you tell? Perhaps when they search it they will say:
"Lady, this suitcase is empty—what were you thinking
     of?"

What was I thinking of? I was going to visit my sister,
Not the one who died, the one who loves and packs well,
And I was going to say goodbye to my Mother (who
     carried
Silk dresses over her arm the time she flew to St. Jo):
I was going to ask—confused and cloudy as where
The planes go—to ask for something to bring you.
Yes, I know I am late and slow packing. I wander, you see.

When they search me I will say: I wander.
Will they take me away then or take the caramel cake
My Grandma baked and that I know I packed carefully?

Sisters, lonely adventurers wave at departure gates,
Planes stack the stormy air outside like cords of wood
In the woodyard at St. Jo: my boarding pass is crimson
As a cloud. I can see you are childless, there are no
Children on the concourse waiting, no reminders

Of tomorrow there or here: only the past,
Silk or rough wool over its arm, jostles us
From the childhood room where we began to pack
Ribbons, tickets, foibles, knives wrapped in cardigans—
Rebellions, clouds, old recipes for shame or love.

I wander. I choose to wander, though, luggage
Full or no luggage at all. The visit behind me,
My gifts are given. Now I remember.
I was going to find one thing more—a crystal of sugar
Or snow for you. (Please don't stop waving.) That is why
I am breathless, waiting to board, awaiting
    the sharp ascent, waiting to go.

On the Night of the Day the World Ends

If we must die
Let us lie one last time
Like a coastline
    glimmering
And the sea
Joined in silvery debris
    and litter of light
All the long way to the world's end:

Let us lie past Time
As shining waves die
    sighing out our banns
And our names die,
Drams of joy lost
    in dried-out fields
With all that will be lost:

If we must die
Let us lie past separateness
Where lineage of the light we bore
    will seed all vanishing
And requite our end
    with stars
Like children safe in space,
Whose parents loved
    and at the last,
  Most brilliantly, were wed.

Consolation

As for consolation, be hard, there is none.
This birth, that death, this fire, that snow
Arrive and are always arriving. Nothing recedes.

What is already here, a pinewood fire or snow,
A raw child or an old man wrapped in snow,
Comes forward, snow blurring fire and birth, death.
Be hard. The fiery wedge of a child arrives
To join death like a green soaked log afire
In a snowy burned-out wood. Old wise men hold
The burning child burns unforgotten, grows
Less and less obscure through rotting snow.
Nothing recedes. Our grief comes forward, riding
On carbon waves of days to carve cold piney shores
Where necessary welcomes hide. But consolation?
There is none. Be clear and hard. Only
That death, this birth, light snow and fiery age
    arrive, arriving always.

The Village Anna

I

Anna
The part in your thick hair lies crooked
As the road that leads out, chalk-white
And unsure, from our village.

Young, rural and bored, your mind wavers:
Lured by mountains to explore, to climb
Over wet snow and violets, lured by horizons

To grow out of the rope belt at your waist
And go far—you wait alone on the road,
Scared and bemused. Mountains beckon,

Mountains bar you from hardship, knowledge and love.
Messages you can't read fall like grain
From the beaks of wild birds.

II

Your eyes, like all eyes ringed by bone
As you are by mountains, go from grain
To star slowly; their glance is narrow.

No deep wells remain outside the valley
Where clear reflections grow into thought,
Or parched hearts seize new meanings of well:

For our sakes you must draw sparkling dark water
From secret sources below the village field;
For our sakes welcome the star in the pail
        with luminous wet eyes.

III

The doors of your body wait to open
On white dawns that bore you: Later,
Distance will fold open, and open shelves

Hold living roots and golden plums
In jars, born from the home fields
To furnish our homesick minds. Tissue

Flowers that rose in the burial ground
Will burn on your hearth like blue
Undergrowth in a clearing in the wind.

Doors will stand open, exciting the fire.
Then who knows how love will fare
Among the populations of your mind.

IV

Outside, we are waiting. Wary solutions
Leap in our hands like pigeons or like guns,
Their blue feathers, blue smoke trailing away.

Promises, stray hopes, white dust of broken roads
Through lost villages, rise to alert and confuse you
Slogging through snow-soaked violets up

To study distance with your opening eyes.
Our waiting wavers. But your waiting
Has a womb, a memory of wells.

V

Anna
Our hearts, like grains of wheat
Tossed down, beat to know if a village
Can be transported over mountains:

If you will read the red-gold messages
Found in isolated fields, and be transported:
If your roots will provide rainy vines

To refresh our cities; and your lazy mind,
Shocked alive this lonely dawn, will open
New meanings of well to revive our waiting:

If you will travel the chalk-white road
Past blue barriers, out, to welcome birth
At last with a wide and widening glance:

Aware of stars heaped in the dark pail,
If you will overflow to feed our famine
And foretell
How well, how deep and far, transported, we can go.

The Society of Anna

I

Wrapped in a scarlet robe, Anna prepares
For bed. She sets her black rimmed glasses

On a white pad at her side, adjusts
The pleated shade over the yellow lamp

And lifts a thick book to her knees.
There is an apple on a plate, waiting,

And it is dark outside. Anna faces
The night beyond her window; what she sees,

Small on the glass pane, is herself clad
In scarlet silk, holding a black book;

White paper and an apple are waiting.
She lifts her glasses and begins to look.

II

The world outside; the book; Anna
Under the yellow lamp. In time

Answers may narrow to the black point
Of her pen answering the white page.

Is it a world of giants, or of dolls
In lacquered masks playing giant?

Is she backward or brave to spy
Their antics and admit them in?

Are there lakes prone in the night,
Shady and sleek as her mind bent

Over them? Do the night winds contort
Or pacify? Anna is looking, looking.

III

What does the grave book say?
That someone has failed: there is

No blame. Women with lifted faces
Are wasting away. Old courtesans,

Painted children, swarthy mothers,
Attack in silent sisterhoods of rage.

Anna must poll whole precincts
Of their pain before she draws her pen.

What is society? The people crowd
From cubicles to make their claim.

IV
Anna, her face like porcelain
Cracked with worry, leans in scarlet;

Her eyes are seams in the earth
For fire or flowers to break through;

She is stained yellow by light, and
Smeared with dreams. There is old age,

Parchment waiting. Anna dozes, starts
Awake over her book. Reads of her sisters

Whose coruscating wit and fitful
Brilliance are—fireflies on a black lake.

V
A poor scared heroine, Anna hears
The steely whine of machines crying;

Awake, dreams papier maché masks
Askew by chariots with dahlia wheels,

And orange signposts in Urdu:
Prayers splay from the splayed mouths

Of children betrayed and men and women
Wrecked by blame. Weak, not knowing

What to do, Anna scorns crying,
And turns her head away. Be fair, Anna—

VI

There is blame to spare. Why
Do the women complain? Anguish always

Lies alone, and exploration costs
Too much. Anna invites her sisters in:

Eleanor of Aquitaine folded in stone,
Far from the High Place of her loves,

Elizabeth bloody in amethyst; de Staël,
Carnations on her tailored breast,

de Beauvoir cold, rebellious, chaste;
And plain women, helpless as leaves

Blowing West. She is tired of women,
Too lost or lazy for her book.

Still there are salons, hearths, huts
And turrets for everyone. She remembers:

VII
History: how a child in white
Ruffles rammed a plum tree once—

A tantrum of child and blossom.
That child stamped in leather boots

Buttoned with apple seeds; that child,
Rosy, raging, gave to Anna—Anna;

And the night pane, the apple
On a plate to be studied. Ancestors,

Her mother's childhood, white ruffles,
Her own childhood lasting too long.

VIII
A yellow porch light among elms,
A black barberry bush, and a child

In a red silk smock, up late, her hand
In Father's hand reaching for Arcturus

And fireflies to chart and hold
One deep night long ago. That porch light

Blooms like a marigold between her room
And distant talk remembered, about love:

IX
The ongoing simple law he told,
Holding the child, never withholding,

Never judging girls gaudy with pain,
Or torn children or nightmare dwarves

Who peer in steely lakes while snow
Like gauze falls silently over all

Their wounds and wars; slow
In the circle of yellow light

He made a circle with his arm
And told the law of love he knew,

Lost now in crescendos of her blood—
Or have they borne tender words? Glorias?

There is silence everywhere. Silence
Throbs and sighs under the pleated shade.

X
Anna's loves write silently while
Night walls sleep outside; secrets

Never to be told, but known, widen
Over ivy, wood and stone, and

Flesh grown opulent as flowers,
Waking dark unguarded walls

With wild graffiti, silently,
She replies with a bold heart

And flames drawn on the snowy page—
Open secrets laugh at walls:

Anna in scarlet silently
Scrawls L O V E above her melting name.

79

XI
Now children come through the dark,
In the guise of an unwary pride, into

The lamplight. Awed, Anna admires
Her own, but in the name of love

Slowly, lawfully sets them free—
To explore, to refuse, merely

To cry they were damaged?
But surely they will give and give love?

Was it a book she dreamed
That raised them, white pages . . . ?

XII
A monk in saffron robes thrusts
Through the lamplight fiercely.

Soldiers and jungles enter in garbles
Of protest. Gasoline, courage, folly.

The righteous burn; her wrath burns
Righteously; Anna reviles hatred too:

What if the monk were simple and lotus-
Sane? Saffron and fire melt, outrage

And confound her. She sees bronze
Temple bells over her soldier children.

Anonymous, far away in the dark,
The crazed face of her cowardice.

XIII
Anna puts her glasses on. Sweet
To be sane. But sanity she knows,

Seed, root, stem, vein and bud—
That sparkling fruit—ripens slow.

With round strokes on the page
She draws an apple, whole;

She spatters ink for seeds
But cannot see the core.

Her face shines back at her
From the black pane—of course!

That's what a knife is for!
Still, she hates violence.

XIV

Childish Anna. The past behind
The past, engraved in shadow

Under candle wax and black beards,
It silent; cannot advise vast Anna

Nor teach her what is wise. Worlds
In Anna rise; wars outside and in

Wage her. Grandfathers and young loves
Stand by while she alone prepares the feast

She must. Only Anna can prepare.
Only all the naked unmasked Annas

With rose-red apples waiting there
At night on polished plates.

     XV
She must begin: At once and all
At once to learn the lake outside

The pane, her face outside and in;
Her tiny soul turned venturesome;

Dolls, rebels, dahlia suns and sin:
And women weak as she; monumental

Annas who must at last be focused
As the pen that stutters passion down.

She carves her apple clean and bites
Into the core. Jots a line,

Tastes more, and finds that nothing
Is enough. Enough is porcelain

To break. Weary of apple flesh
She rises to her knees, scattering

Book and glasses on discarded silk—
To seize beyond night scars her own,

The outline of her burden drawn
Sharp and clear on the dividing pane;

At once and all at once the unknown
Generous to adore, the seed of wisdom

At the core: In this lone Anna, coward,
Fool, a whole society of Anna born.

THE RIPENING LIGHT

NOTE

You can't find your own hand in the dark?
Don't worry. It is outdoors
Groping over rosebushes
And ochre cliffs to find
A heart awake and waiting
More than a mile away.

Cerro Gordo Dreams

We go aboard
wood-feathered
ancient pine-beaked ships
that sail from Cerro Gordo

nightly

Noah's neighbors   murderous lookouts
ivory heroes and moon-white lovers
cast off and dream
in the green mind
of a sleepless teacher of night music

slowly

iris-eyed figureheads
wreathed in scampi roses   salt tears and sorrow
meet the seas
between dark cedar wings
and sing

then over the rock waves
and wavering peaks of Cerro Gordo
wild doves streak
with boughs of music from silver olive trees
in their beaks dripping light

at dawn

we go down the gangplank
slowly
hope stinging the coral corners of some eyes

As One Gull Holds the Sky

I
aieee
little dancer
the bearded Fathers
charted your blue veins long ago

surveyed the rocks you flow through
to rocky basins
you will overflow one day
dancing
their state of mind

aieee
monumental in the sand
the stern old men
watch you grow

weightless

the motion of your hand
their dying breath a tall young fountain
dancing in time

2
little dancer
who are They?
ankle deep in waves along the shore
watching you dance

landscapes on the air
mountains in flight
and mica deserts quivering
light like water

in provinces of the heart
where they cup massive hands
to drink you

Presences Fathers
who are they
circling slowly round
to observe you

dancing

holding it all together
as one gull holds the sky

The Undistinguished

A heap of pine cones or of men
Dries blood-brown in the sun.
Who can tell, on a day studded
With targets like cloves on the plain,
What matters?

A soldier in brown boots crushes
Pine cones in the brown woods;
A man of power in a nicotine-brown room
Cracks walnuts, and bones for their marrow;
Even cracks mountains. If there are men
On the mountain he cannot see them,
Though he holds glasses in a leather case
As the soldier holds a gun.
Who can tell what matters?

We have nothing but cotton thread
To sew bone buttons on a coat;
Only a room brown as a pine cone,
With a wood bed, and a table

Where bread crusts and a crumb
Assert themselves.

We have only hope, distinct
As one brown aster on the mountain
Far away, kindling the bare eye,
Celebrating all the pine cones,
All the undistinguished men,
All that matters; out of range
Of power or gun, small
And resinous in the sun.

Crudités

an old woman
smears
earth and sweat
together and makes
of her face a garden

then mimes
the climbing bean
and blossom of the squash
with open earth-caked hands

mimes robust ripening

till a smile breaks through
her brown and crusty flesh
to feed us in our millions
to feed us in our anger

simplicity in flower
simple as a pardon

Homestead

Children,
On a cold night under a cold moon,
Mother, holding her old bathrobe closed,
Leaves home. Father, his ankle bones
White spurs over flopping slippers, leaves too.
Why do they run down the cement walk
By the black hedge God gave them to tend
And prune? Chilled by a moon without family,
Why do they run so awkwardly? And where?

Back to bed, go back.
Their secrets are too young for you yet.

Besides, they'll be home before you wake,
Dumping coffee grounds down the drain,
Faces taut or slack with all they've seen
Under a night sky without end. Be proud of them—

Bathrobe and slippers flapping, cold,
Freezing with enterprise, your parents

Explore the night in long forced marches
To unwalled forts and sprawled-out plains
Where promises thrash like black calves
In a sweat of stars. Be still.

Perhaps I'll tell their secret after all—
How, cold to their bones with wonder,
Your parents search the night for a country
Without borders, a wide round clearing
Without an edge they found and lost before.

They will set out again tonight; Mother
To discover the open place inside,
No limit to danger, where she'll settle
Once you're fed; and father, too, be glad,
His own dangerous acre to ride beyond
The clipped hedge, under a lonely moon—
Go back to bed—
Where dreams wilder than you
Colonize
An untamed country,
        their true homestead.

The Ripening Light

Desire waits.
Light pollinates
The slow instinct of season
With promise of a flower
And a pear of reason.
The aging tree debates,
Winter on its tongue,
Why passion takes so long;
If darkness will create
A dark and wizened fruit.
But under leaves of snow
Desire burns and waits,
Sure that the light-loved
Tree will bear
The flower and a radiant pear.

Sari

once
in a sari like a flame
holding a naked child
by one brown hand
she moved across the plain

the light was bronze

she was going to the well
for water
or to the river
to bathe her son
and pour laughter
from a tall jar over him
in the drought of our eyes

in the bronze light

now by the dried-out well
and river that are gone

gold bracelets round the arm
that holds her naked son
she turns
our thirst demands
she turn
black eyes raining
answers though they burned
long ago

and long ago
we cast that sari   child   and flame
for our dry age to drink from them
the light

the light is bronze

Response to a Night Wind

The river comes down in the dark.
Wind beaten by stones comes
From Tibet through gorges of silence
Filled in our minds by bells
And by men broken on stones
      foaming down
To carve mountains (we need never climb)
      out of darkness.

Torn prayer rags waver at cold cave doors,
While sure as crystals of sorrow
      born on the wind,
Sure as torrents of men or beaten bells
      ringing silence somewhere,
The river comes down in the dark

To measure our sleep and our waking,
      prayer by prayer.

On a Phrase by Camus

A philosopher one night
In a room stripped nearly bare,
Sorted the wars he'd won,
The debts to the past he owed,
Then set his mind alight
To shine on darkened lives;
And beyond rebellion prayed
For a "lucid heart,"
And died.

In our reddish littered room
Where the bed's brass flowers
Climb, his words flame from
The page of the anguished book
We hold—ruby as vigil lights
Or rayed young blood
On walls grown radiant
And dark denied;

Out of the space he found
And out of the ways he lost
He shaped lamp and edifice;
And what he sent at last
From his wide, illumined
Mind, was a phrase—a wick
Of discipline and praise
For obscure lives he shared
And clarified.

The world he had tried
To light with his own devout
Dissent, receives beyond despair
A branch of living fire
To bear in bowls of night:
His lucid heart
In flower—
His death, our deaths
Defied.

Painting with Child

Night the mother, father fire,
Breed morning children in the dark.

Alone, she draws a cradle arc,
Tucks in snow and braids a flame

To welcome their gold flickering,
Then paints a sunrise on the floor

With ochre, quartz, and crimson ore,
Ground bone of owl and honeycomb—

As conch and drumbeat tell the dawn
Why night and fire lie on stone,

And she grows warm with child again.

A Dream of Peaches

1
During pregnancy and war

They reach for peaches in a clay bowl
And remember orchards—

Red hump-backed leaves when peaches were ripe
Under the rosy cliffs of the Canyon de Chelly
Or by a brown house late one summer.

They rub rough bark, rub leaves
And the furred curve of the fruit.
Though clay bowls and skulls shatter daily
They focus on
Cloves, gold latticed cobblers, brandied juices.

2
Some peaches are bird-beaked
And blemished by August though they hang on.

A brown retriever running by tramples
One perfect peach on the ground.

Wasps, unplayful, shrewish and shrewd,
Market thriftily among brownish pulp.

A blue-jeaned boy on the housetop
Hurls peaches down like bombs
To splash open on bare dirt below.

A little girl sorts peach pits reverently,
Prods them with a stick into sandy soil
And spits like her brother, to start trees.

3
Kerchiefed women hold baskets
And brown-handled rakes. Later,
Peaches dried on the roof in the sun
Will yield iron
For dreams to chew in the lean winter days.

4
Think of peaches in winter
When the fire is lit
And women in sable
Shadows
Sit squandering strength and pointed stories,

Little silver sharp knives in their hands.

Perhaps there is still a war going on.

Think of women without fruit bowls
Or fretful fires, their knives glittering
Like rain in rooms too dark for shadows.

Perhaps they are pregnant.

In some rooms pain takes up what room there is
And stands out clearly.

5
Mothers-to-be
Loll on striped chairs in the sun,
Grown ravenous for adoration
In whole orchards of their own:

Older children, noisy
Boys and girls who tackle beauty,
Fumble the prize and cry out,
Run by—

Fear kicks.

Once they wore blossoms in their hair.
Now through veils of summer heat,

Dreams of wasp-waists and flowers,
The women lurch awake, detergent, strong,
Strict eyes open
To punish malingerers.

6
One pregnant woman stands by a bowl full of peaches.

The sky is sapphire over war
And white orchards.

Too tired for satire or scorn,
She possesses nothing anymore

But memory and hope
Like a rope of white rain

Lashing sky and life together.
Slowly, stroking the gold peaches,

She prepares for changes
To possess her—perhaps

To feast on her ripening dreams—
But frugally, since she is pregnant still

And beyond the orchard there is war.

From the Loom of Juniper Woman

1

The weaver of the story is Juniper Woman.
A cloud in a winter sky groping for spring,
The story is also a landscape with willows,
An arroyo stream, a man like stone in ice,
Danger, unsheathed knives, and the sound
Of marriage bells. Young girls wearing wooden
Crowns in a town the size of a hand holding
A gold ring are woven in.

2

It is all related slowly, with natural dyes—
Walnut for lava mesas and indigo for skies split
By black lightnings. A red sunset, cochineal,
Arcs over lovers, masked clowns and antlered
Dancers bending to graze the dark woolen ground.
Knotted muscles and clots of fear,
The textures of bark and fur, the flesh

Of leaves and of suffering, of lives formal as asters
Growing from rock, and abnormal as sanity, are
     woven in.

3
Juniper Woman holds the story in her hands
In silence, the skein and the dyed wools,
Slowly weaving together the cloudy old
Who bargained for hemlock or healing, and
The treacherous young caught on barbed
Thorns of wild ochre roses—all to emerge
Clear in the design, the story bordered by
Poplar spears guarding dark clans of pine
By bridal streams that dance in the firelight.

4
Where later a wand of fire falling through the night
Will reveal Juniper Woman still at her loom, weaving
The dreams of other weavers who sleep. We see her
Framed in that place before dawn, laughing, the weaver
Of the story, calm and complete.
What wisdom there is, is hers
As she throws the flickering blanket down
     to be walked on.

There Will Be One to Focus On

For a grandchild

Little one,
when all the people gather—
all the pods, stalks, weeds and sunflower
faces gather in a place common
to all on a road lined with early ice
and police afraid of common faces
like threatening weeds without names—

even among so many you will see,
shining here and there in the crowd
soiled by events and stained
with the waiting that sweats
in any season, city or field,
through every language or gesture,
every lift of a gun or face
lined with patience lifted
in the gathering of common faces—
will see that rarity,

the unmistakable presence
so carved by grace it can be seen
shining among the others, though
it does not stand taller nor step
forward. It is there, he or she
there, a great artisan of the spirit

waiting among the anguished faces,
the slow explosion of plain humanity
gathered
to face that other explosion coming—
a radiant spirit on the road alone
among many, shining out to sustain you
as sun sustains an upturned sunflower face—

child, find suffering's most noble one
        to focus on . . .

Before the Light Is Steady

at dawn
Juniper takes another's sorrow in her hand

a shard or splinter of red rock
from arroyo bed or red dawn mountain

to weigh against her own hard pain
before the light is steady

over calm mesas or abominations
of far wars staining deserts

similar to hers, staining
other lives and agonies red-coral

as the rock she flings up to
today's uncaring peak runneled

by a fresh erosion of tears
on cliff faces and faces accustomed

to tears; the suffering of others mighty,
their sorrows weighty, outweighing her own

before the light is steady
in Juniper's cupped hand   humble and red

at dawn

At Pilar for K.

Listen
There are two lives I want to tell you about
By the silent cedars and the still brown water
Near Pilar. Between gouged rock
And sunflowers on the shore,
Two lives to tell. The river
Lies still and lava hills frown down
On fragrance—of bay? Of juniper?
Somewhere near here long ago
Two lives held hands and spoke
Of you with love. Listen

Today only fragrance speaks

"Exposed on the Cliffs of the Heart"

—*Rainer Maria Rilke*

a deer   a stalking man
who blesses the deer
humbly before the kill

and sheer against red rock
the figure of a woman
blessing deer and man

on a cliff carved out
by air and assaulted
by strangers' eyes

like obsidian arrowheads
sharpened to pierce
an indistinct past alive

again   the antlered deer
running still and the taut
hunter poised forever

motionless for the kill
against red rock blurred
by rain where rain-veiled

the woman mourns old ways
grown vague—old blessings
streaked with fresh blood

as scared strangers climb
through lightning air
awed   at hazard too

exposed forever
on the red cliffs of the heart

Juniper After Rain

after the rain Juniper Woman
shakes out tiered skirts
and three birds from the twin pines

picks up her day
in its wet basket
young lilac from the clay pit
a red chief's blanket

and sets out
plodding
past the friend's house
where they discuss
   conquest and ease

no friendship
thin as her hair
or as gramma grass on the cliff
can turn her aside

oh no after rain
she huddles her basket along

lilac stretched like a cat
on the folded red blanket
stroked by dry light

she's going to steal
a white dime of rain
caught in a vise of rock
not thinking

of conquest and ease
friendship
or us   why should she

wrong to expect an answer
when she's so busy

Wild Geese

They listen
To geese in midpassage over the glassy pond
And icy grasses, honking their way, a winged "V"
Through storm. On the ground, woman

After woman stands with hood thrown back
To watch the pointed flight, assurance overhead,
Parting gray light as she parts tangled hair

Over the ache of wonder and the perverse fear—
Now she holds seasons in her mittened hand
To mend or ravel or reverse at will—

The fear of morning, cold and irresponsible,
Thrusting against her narrow unchanged bed
An insistent clutter of torn loves and chores.

"Thy will be done," but "Duty to self alone,"
One says; her words, like seeds, an anarchy
That spreads bright spores to hooded minds, all

Longing to conform. So woman after woman walks
On ice to peer up through the snow and hear
The coarse cries of wild geese bound for

Far kinder air. The season of her will
Seeded with choice, stunned now and released,
Each woman bears the wild impact of that instinctive
Flight—above her puny storm, the great formation's
weight.

Parade

Dancers
crowned with peach buds
march on satin club feet
through the sand

a woman shaped like a fir tree
wound with green wind rolls by

streams of faces
nostrils like black silver
sniff the cold air

tracking the dancers
on their way to the mesa

to praise? to protest?

climb with us
past floats
trimmed with unborn lilac

and clacking cockroach shells
past gargoyles and clowns
        dragging
a painted saint on wooden wheels

to the flat mesa top
where black goats crop
below the hawks' pas de deux
this raw May day

help us retie the green ribbons

stand back   stand back
let the dancers clump on their way
to protest or praise

cold day
so many crowns in bud
all that pain all that joy
parade without end
        hobbling by

Weaver, Weave Sun

Juniper Woman
weave sun and wool
into the color of leaves
autumn leaves
changeable as old loves

faces upturned
or downcast under a sky
carded umber and still

till silver winds
reveal
each leaf and face
individual
shaken, shriveled, thin
nothing but lace vein
and bronze-spotted skin
left to cherish

hanging on against dark
dark clouds woven in
but with a rich glint still

old leaves, old loves
precarious and beautiful

With Horror, Sir, Sincerely

Sir:

It is dark still as the trucks
Loaded with apples and beef press on
Past Algodones, beaded with lemon-colored
Lights in the cold before dawn, and I begin
To write with cold hands, before dawn, at my table.

I want you to know I am loyal,
Not just to my orchard and pine trees
By a slate-colored pond, but to other pines
Far away in gaunt lonely stands, or guarding
Kerchiefs of lawn where it is already light
And men and women, to whom I am loyal too, set out for
    work.

Forgive me, the fire won't start
In the black stove; I am cold with alarm.
My mind follows those trucks as though
They were schooners, yellow oil lamps

In the rigging, beating out, braving it
Over asphalt waves and over our mountains,
The drowsy men on watch waiting for
Steamy breaks and wedges of gray apple pie
At a stop past dawn and Algodones.

For their sakes my mind slows over the cold curve
Of my hand. Sir, I am afraid, and though
Loyal, afraid to say why. There is coffee
On my stove and cold bacon in a pan.
Sir, I have a message from us all.

Once I saw a flock of geese cross paths
With a jet plane. White bloody
Carcasses, red feathers, steel and flesh
Falling on this valley explode my sleep still.
No, that is not the message: merely an event
No wise man could foresee. But mindless
Events, like geese and jet, like kinds of pride
Collide, and good minds streak, mindless,
To disaster. I know there has been an explosion, sir,
And that various kinds of wings, like greatness,
Fall. That is not my message.

After all, I only want to say: Wrong's wrong.
Out here as trucks rush past on black
Macadam waves before morning, you could sit
With me, knowing coldly who wronged the drivers
And us all.

THE RIPENING LIGHT

There are feathers and steel,
Untasted bacon, wasted men and trucks
Whose gears broke as they rode to destinations
Everywhere in the land this morning.
It is seven now. My hand warms, and its curves
Warm into anger and grief
Beside the yellow danger signs. Wrong's wrong.
Honor lies wrecked along this road
And stands of pines; and history, History shouts
Out over the land like dawn. Face it.

There are chores to be done, so I must close.
Beyond maimed hopes and bloodied minds,
Beyond Algodones even, I remain, with horror, sir,

        Sincerely.

Lovers' Warning

The birds are everywhere in the air this morning.
Brown-ruffed, with bronze or rusty shields
On their breasts, slight warriors climb
The air to the fir tree top, wheeling,
Preparing for—who knows—jet steep
Descents into a day crisscrossed
By feathered rumors, tossed here and there
Against clouds grown momentous
Over the tousled heads of boys,
And lovers in quilted robes staring
Out, unable to assess war or weather,
Unarmored so far, so early—

A brown apricot leaf like a butterfly
Blown to a pine tree needle and
Sewn crudely in place, rests
Before the birds swoop again
And upturned faces turn away, wiping
Dark interrogations from their eyes,

Murmuring, "They say it is coming,
The birds can't find their way,
What does it mean? What can we do?"

Assailed, old lovers sort and gather
Other commotions of wind and wing
To narrate, old invasions that were
Mounted once—bloody incursions into
Landscapes shaken past ripeness—they
Remember the repeated warnings of beaten
Brothers, old farmers, old mothers
With lackluster eyes on ruined harvests,

And children restless to be grown and going
To war again. Aware, unaware of commentaries
Overheard this morning, of retreats and charges,
The tremendous air bearing down as before,
Starlings off course bearing news; another
Invasion somewhere coming silently near

While the leaf like a butterfly trembles
On the shaken tree and those who watch
Shake under wings out of formation,
Confused as blown leaves falling, without
Pattern, commander or base, before
Full light and clear apprehension
For those who walk on legs, hold hands,
Stroke a child's head and ask what to do,

Shaking as they read wing points' clear
Warnings blurred into cloud, reading the blood
That repeats in their veins repeating
Someone may fire soon

BEWARE

The Day the Decision Was Taken

In that light, in that wind, on that morning
something was decided. The pine trees
drew closer, the man and the woman drew
closer in bed again, sensing
something grave in the air, sensing
something had occurred overnight, before dawn,
in a cave under the Rockies—and it was true—
in a brain in that cave the decision was taken,
though the mountains continued to kneel
for a time, and pine trees like priests
bowed their heads over lovers, lost souls
and madmen with crocus words ready to bloom
till something, the last denial of spring
set its seal and became known, leaked
like rain everywhere—to evergreen roots,
to lovers and bearers of love grown barren
who wept, once what was decided was known,
beyond terror in one frieze of hopeless grace,
one springlike wide embrace, vulnerable
and aware, already lost in that light,
　　　　that rising wind, that fatal dawn

Squirrel

now let us celebrate the day
like any other day when the white
(almost white in the sun) squirrel
posed on the sharp roof ledge
above wood corbels carved long ago

stood on his hind legs, thin claw hands
held out in benediction or malediction,
we couldn't tell which, over the white heat
of a drought day like any other
when the throats of mourning doves
dried in the sun by noon, the flowers
shook and looked white, there were rumors
of riots or rain that refused to come,
asbestos was lodged in the lung, and fat
granaries exploded; a day when plague
announced itself again in a dead coyote
furring the naked ground, and butterflies,
dark eyelets in their open wings, worked
drying clover at the desert's edge—

celebrate the squirrel on the roof
stock still and odd in the white light

potent with blessings or danger,
we don't know which, fixed there over
warning signs we still can't read, carved
black shadows clawing the old corbels.

The Fox and the Flood

O quiet quiet as the fox through the bush
without leaves watches April rain and a house
slide quiet down the white and watchful dawn

the arroyo runs with news, skies betray and run
April into May over the fox's eye, and the bare
bush pulls at its root to outrun O quietly

catastrophe so common now even the hidden fox
senses something wrong, a season running away
and certainty awash—the fox hunts us or will,

bristling dry from the chilly brush, old burnished
fox aware of sly rumor air spreads freely, prowls
the flooded quiet where tyrants and rebels rise

and the carved white cornice falling, cries
take me swiftly down, twined with roots of bay
to the running familiar clay but quiet quietly—

through the blind rush sucking what used to be
fair destroyed and light leaves torn away
to crown both naked May and the wary fox at dawn
        posed glistening in the waste.

When You Sleep You Grow

I
in the night overnight in sleep
in the rise and ebb of the soul's tides

in minute scratchings of rain on rose windows
tiny claws on icons afloat in dark oceans
in the brain the motionless body or room
unseen motions change rise and swirl
nightly

yesterday's triumph over loss, lost
yesterday's virtue and love lost too

in the night of the clouded brain
in the window closed to moonlight and wind
betrayals and fine tunings are made
tiny creatures looking down scratch sound
from tin bells ringing soundless over
cave-ins and sea changes in windy naves
lined with white moon faces praying
against change as change roils on

in the night   in the sleep of one
transformed like everyone else nightly

they used to say that when you sleep you grow

all we know after grave turmoil
is that day comes daily according to the law
to create itself again, grimed or sparkling
at our windows

2
. . . it is created again today
out of the caverns of sleep

where the yellow-faced inquisitor
stirred blood with his toe
and the opulent great sagged
like dwarves in guttural shadows
lit here and there by miners' lamps

on faces charcoal-gashed
as Dachau's dead, on the sallow
faces of lackeys, Rouault saints
and clowns merged in the dark
confluence of sleep

in ancient caverns where
the "born again" stab

with their knives at stalactites
of hanging men or poor men
lost in history's sinkholes
knee deep in guano and bearing
mean banners through the ashy dark

till a vast stretching, blinking, licking
away of the nightmare begins, and for some
a landscape fragrant with cedar
opens and sunlight opens again
on the miracle that announces
it is all created again today—

and our reply? plainly our reply must be:
we too are present

Shiprock

Where begging hands arch the hot aisles
And the desert prays crudely, no angel faces
Part the burning clouds, no guild of lovers
Carves the parapets with bloom;
Only sun thunders down and the loud
Wings of a bird assault the heat-cowled
Presence of the Stone.

We who made lenses of the burning sands,
Who see with our making hands, failed
Tests of vision, worship's tool,
By forcing nature's holy will
Into the glass our reason fused—
Now lightnings shatter seeds of rock,
Roots explode in booming light, and
Dreams we built crash to their knees.

Who formed this Carcassonne of Stone
Where sun astounds and halos burn
Over the last unyielding spires;

THE RIPENING LIGHT

Where cold as granite angels' eyes
Our eyes once charged the potent aisles?
We kneel, and with the desert pray
For wings and clarity to bloom,
For the stone Presence to persist—

Our hands gone blind with wonder
Whose wonder broke Creation's fist.

The Level Eye

When I say willows are dying
by the dry stream beds
and people are moving away
I mean trees are dying
everywhere and day by day
water is sinking back
to strata in the rock
no one can reach

and the people
(they are what matters)
the people like willow leaves
coated with silver on one side
lie too tarnished and dry
for love, or to reach
water drawing away
out of reach everywhere

what I mean falls
like a stone in the sand

where people and water
(they are what matters)
go on moving and drawing away
from each other and farther
and deeper each day

and who will dive down
to find their sunken
silver ghosts together at last?
I mean who will be left
to drink a lonely toast
to all that mattered
around the glittering table in the dark?

Juniper for Our Sakes

I
Juniper Woman, stranger,
you walk among us in your red rebozo,
old and sinewy, hiding the landscape
that lives behind your eyes
    fenced with bone—

disdainful, not of our burial mounds
spread all the way to the last mesa,
but of our living pride—young

warriors in leather helmets massed
like fall cottonwood leaves in the wind,
beaten
before they begin to search and destroy
the desert canyons of the heart

where your wide eyes once corralled
a red mare, a man in a headband
dancing for rain, a season of trust—

2
Juniper for our sakes
teach our sons how to herd
wild dreams with green willow manes

teach them to live dying of thirst
when white suns attack, by licking
secret water from the canyon sand
they stormed; teach them to snare and kill

the running hare or diamondback,
and with scant piñon boughs to build
ramadas for their savaged pride—

Juniper let your eyes speak landscapes
where the young can survive

hunkered down
in the shelter of your red rebozo
as by a hidden fire
to strip bones bare and chew
            the raw integument of truth

The Sybil at Market Time

"Words are dying and will be dead soon,"
She warns, her hand on the linen page,
Drawing swords and famous faces,
And with the steel point of the pen,
Pointed words in crowns of oak leaves.

Then, "Old men, hide your young
Before spring. Spring is the time
For dismembering," she writes, smiling,
A sybil brown as an autumn pod, dry
And feathered with pride. That done,
Ponders a shapely market list: melon,
Curved tongue, onions to braise,
Dark wrinkled raisins, Lux. LUX!

Light traipses across the windowsill
Trailing an acrid yellow smell
Of marigolds. Her hand falls silent;
Then poised and listening, lifts
The pen again to make the LUX black
And ornate, and print beside her glistening
Name, in a pungent frame of marigolds,
A young and lurid question mark.

The Great Are Called

I
called

they will come on a day
that drips light like honey
over deserts and starved gardens

the great ones, each extreme
in greatness as a cardinal
in his cloak, cabochons flashing

each face an occasion
each fame hard as the base
of a statue splintered by ice—
condescending or kind
will come to aid or silence us,
the hungry others, our bowed spines

weak as silk, begging
for great answers like alms
from the minds of the mighty

till water breaks in the fountain
and new eminences storm forth
from the cloister of old bones
daring to pray   or answer for us

called

2
who are they, the great ones?

unknowns
cowled in secret grandeur
or idols in splendor
sequin on sequin
contrived by our eyes
to perform
glittering beyond praise?

those who untongued you
and strung you up by your heartstrings
gory with song?

or the humble ones
in anonymous dark
beyond arc lights
binding those same heartstrings

with bloodied strands of dawn—

who are they?   name them
the truly great
who torture you
by withholding nothing

glory
the color of a kernel of corn
in their morning hands

Akhmatova

In the evening
To make light of her suffering

Akhmatova set a lamp in the window
By three green apples
On the splintered sill, and said:

" . . . if I could step outside myself
And contemplate the person that I am
I should know at last what envy is. "

Wry lamplight bronzed the apples;
Our arrogance denied her pride.

But Akhmatova, indomitable, survived
Years of frozen nights like prison walls
To reach us, shining.

Now dark descends, we step outside
To contemplate the poet that she was—

A lamp set in a window,

A bright wick soaked in joy
Like diamond oil—and suffering vivid

As the smell of a hand that held apples
Held out still
To illumine and forgive
Our envy, lustrous
And calm as bronze at last
In light of the light she gave.

No Lineage but Light

She has come to stay awhile
In a work dress red as willow stems,
The scent of resin on her hands.
Being a no one, a foundling,
She will work for nothing but love.

She brings a light bundle
Of ironed ribbons and laughter,
And a singing bird in a basket.

"Which would you rather have,"
She asks, "A hand
Or a wing
In your hand?"

"It depends . . ." we say, trying
To earn her.

Fiercely she scours the hearthstone
With columbine-white soapsuds,

While the bird,
Flecks of seriousness in its eyes,
Sings.

"It depends," we say, depending on her,
As with sanity and passion, she opens
Dark cupboards and feeds the bird
Fresh songs from high shelves.

If we earn her
The apple logs she sets aflame
Will burn on the hearthstone
With the wild fragrance of fidelity
To steady us

When she is gone,
A no one,
No lineage but light.

Your Face with Tiger Lilies

For A. P. W.

Your face leans over mine
in the basin of the fountain

tiger lilies stolen from the cemetery
long ago in one hand and in the other
an unwritten book—I can't see the title.
Are we still friends?

Your crinkled hair is wet; a lie
like an adventure outlines your narrow lips
in the clear brown fountain water.

After the Nova Scotia affair
you wrote from African deserts
where "tawny lions mate by moonlight,"
then, your own midwife, bore and lost
twins—then silence. Years later
I heard you died, willfully, of starvation
in an eastern city.

You had said, "I want to be unknown
as a grain of sand in the desert."
Another lie, of course, but prophetic.

Now here you are, brilliant with tiger lilies,
tawny adventures, an invisible book in your hand,
your pale illumined face overshadowing mine
in the basin of the fountain. Are we friends?

I'd know you anywhere.

The Breaking Apart

After the break dance and the parting,
The TV hero's pleas for war
        and the parting
Of soldiers and lovers into sleep—

Others are on the move at night,
Going neither secretly nor with stealth
But unseen and soft to spare and honor
The sleepers, the closed wild roses,
The nested birds quiet in high trees;
Searching late and alone through the dark
For a face like a meadow to graze—
Surely somewhere there is a meadow
Of stars and of faces that flower
Like stars, to share beyond parting?
For those spirits on the move at night
Hope is the mystic brute
That may or may not lead in time
To the face and the field that shine
Among tall trees of the sleeping world
For this throng of quiet ones, faithful

Beyond tomorrow's dark armed promise,
Beyond tomorrow's inevitable
        breaking apart

To The Approaches

We can't say what "The Approaches" are, though we seem to have stumbled into them.

The Approaches are . . . age,
the years the child saw far ahead
in a distance too blinding bright
to enter, and that she learned about too late;

but here we are, they are, the years,
the approaches blazing like summer roads
we set our bare or booted feet upon,
our calloused dancing or warrior feet

on roads like arrows blunted by time,
that speed nevertheless beyond
laurel leaves and strong laureled loves
to discs of fiery blood within

discs of white light at the heart;
the unknown target that we sight,
that the child within us stands
before, an untrained archer, lame,

with muscles torn and eyes that strain
past bloodied asphalt or darkening white
dust; a clumsy child learning again
to focus close-up on wonder—on a bright

serrated rose leaf or an uncertain love—
ailing or dancing now, here, alone in
the approaches, feet booted or bare,
feeling earth beneath the stance

we will each take at last,
each child a great athlete of sorrow
aimed at that disc of absolute white light.

Only

only sky
through a hole in the fence

a slow movement of air
stirring clouds bunched
like cows by bare trees
in rivers stately and vague

only a dark dab of a child
a pinafore
a round straw hat
veiled with rain
bowing eye to eyehole

a slow movement of years
a slow leafing of air
an old mind blurred by rain
twining leaves to wear
dancing
over rain-soaked stone

beyond the fence

only the brilliant stare
of the quick child
moving near—

the bold past sashed with light

To Become a Dancer

To become a dancer so late
To be determined so late to become
A dancer is to become part
Of the dream of the humble heart
Determined to dance to the beat
Of this one dawn becoming day
Caught by a great blush and throb
Of laughter at such a becoming
Such a desire to become a dancer
In the sense of one moving, clumsy
With effort, yet effortlessly becoming

The limbs of the old tree bent
Out of shape and dancing, leaf-bare
On a windless day before snow,
Becoming the bent shape of itself—
That sort of dancing, of sensing
With alert heart the snow-blurred
Motion or natural pause of tree
And of woman too, weary

And trembling with effort near
The aspen fence or morning barre
Stretching to become what she is
Or may be, laughing down at legs
Wrapped in wooly snow; grim,
Laughing and determined beyond pain
So late to translate at last
Life into life, the shared beat
Of laughter and grief into motion
Part of the dream-game *I dare you*
Accepted

As the reddening curtain rises
The grand jeté of dawn
And silent-as-snow applause rise
To celebrate one so modest and arrogant
Who dares so late, laughing,
To become a great dancer,
That is to say
To become, in a sense, one with the dawn
Beginning

Amulet Songs

I
Red coral in the hand
We sing
Because she was
And is and yet will be
Part of the lullaby
Darkened or lilting grace
We must learn to face
Before shadows robed in white
Rustle at our door
With ampoules on a tray

Lullaby you are
The face that we compose
In spite of what we know
So we in turn can face
The dark we learned from her

Give us the heart to bear
A lamp that sings at night
Across a breast of snow

2
Amulet
Let her wake
One time again to dream
The flaunt of rose-ribbed silk
And pale persimmon light
That dressed an afternoon
Trailing in to meet
Love long ago at home
Her power still alive
And beauty satisfied
In a gold past smocked with gold

Then croon the fire down
Lie if you must lie
Until she lies at peace
Draped in a gown of song
And rich soft folds of stone

You

When afternoon
comes through the red tulip

Sun comes through a hand
like your hand stroking
my head at sunset after pain

To have known
one radiant kind man
is like owning a red tulip
or an afternoon
that lets the light through

The Last Day

Let it come
When buff and gold clouds
Part on lovers and friends
Laughing
Across a clay jar full of sunflowers.

Let it come
When clean hair is braided
And those we love
Are home for a glass of wine
Set out by sunflowers
On the bare wood table;

When old hopeful men
Watching the shadow of the spray
On dry autumn grass
Remember
Wise decisions or folly
In pine forests long ago,
And laugh;
And when the growing children
Have said "No" to fear
Or to something false
And can laugh again;

When bells ring out
In the late afternoon
To celebrate
Resolve and tenderness
Circled by silver-breasted birds;

When the least of us
Gleams from a sturdy bowl of self;
Leaves of basil lie
On clear sauces, water sparkles
In waiting baths, and clean
Rough sheets are laid ready
On our beds;

When the light is a sunflower
In a house opened to hold
Laughter and light,
And we are no longer torn
By needing to go out
Or stay in, no longer afraid
To forgive our own errors . . .

When the spirit is ready,
When everything is ready,
Fresh and simple—
As achieved and plain
As sunflowers
In a jar reddened by sun,
Then let it come.

THE RIPENING LIGHT

THE PINK MADONNA ❧

Papyrus

Little One
small bright parcel of sun
        in the dark

parchment-bound
ancient infant tight-wound
        by light
like papyrus strips torn
open and ready to rise now

from the rushes to requite loss
among hard waves of days
        carved out
around your bloodied cradle
it is early yet   time still

to unwind what binds you
in Time to grow tall   free
        as a stylus

inscribing on dry linen pages
a liquid babble of syllables

that song risen inside you
from an amber-dark past
        lacquered with sun

Little One small parcel of light
small naked gift emerging   live
from broken waters and torn
tissue   History too   breaks
        open to ink Dark

over Sun over Dark   little scribe
waiting like Day itself waiting

to issue forth in Time again
a warm live child ready to be
        unwrapped and poured over—
tomorrow's message   shared
before we risk daring you to live

        daring to let you go

"Arduous Times"

Long ago, Child, a wolf-pack sky loped in
Over black apple trees, barnyards,
And the frozen courtyards of Provence—

Over small timber houses, small torn
Hearts and bones crumbled by fear.

Wiser now, we know wolves mean no harm;
Unlike us, they "attack only when starving."

Still we stand too much at bay, too gnawed
By uncertainty not to turn on them when sky howls

Winter, gray snow covers naked apple trees
In rutted farmyards and grows menacing,

And a furred head appears at the window
Outlined in ice; then the family cringes

Famished and fearful, raw fear sucking

Its marrow. As the old wolf-pack sky lopes

Near again, we fumble for lights and knives,
Shouting alarm; and our old seigneur, old
Broken man, cries over the frozen courtyard here,

"I tell you, these, too, are arduous times . . ."

L'École des Rêves Joyeux

I

Little One, as soon as your blue uniform
Is buttoned and the Light, le Soleil, Sun
Adjusts itself over elm allée and macadam

Where dun-faced chores and children
In stained pinafores stand waiting,
It will be time to start your day's Devoirs . . .

II

In that one day, Little One, you will
Grow, matriculate, wed, give birth,
Bake bread and hold a funeral urn—You!

An explorer advancing, at first alone,
On your long journey from Convent dreams
Into the Light, le Soleil, Sun perhaps . . .

III

Later you will assure your rosy daughter
You made the journey for her sake alone;
True or not, will claim you straddled

Two fierce blue continents to discover
The one habitable one inside, concealing
Only how you filled old frozen diaries

Of your pride with tales of rotted
Sealskins and torn hide tents—
Your lofty inexperience racing forward

IV

To cross the last crevasse—where
You no longer ache to be known,
But exhausted, yearn finally to Know—

Sprawled in a dream tent, so blind
You mistook its chapel dark for Clarity—
The radiant continent you could map

And guide her to, somehow surviving
On bloody seal meat and bird bones
Chewed to feed the marrow of the common
          name you shared . . .

V

Little One, as soon as your blue uniform
Is buttoned, the Light, le Soleil, Sun
Will ease what you most feared, racing

From safe sumac Autumns to alcohol-blue fires
On the long-ago of that wintry expedition
Over tracks black as flayed bark scarring

Hard snow, whose arêtes pierced both you
And your child-to-be—and fear, that melanoma
Of the spirit, rose through lesions in the ice . . .

VI

Before the end, Little One, issue to your snowy child
A warning, a tiny red "blessure" that yields a sample
Of raw tissue to a glass slide of ice beginning to melt . . .

Dire directions toward what may become
For her a sturdy transience—your courage,
Her safe passage under the flag of a benign
     and arduous joy . . .

VII

Aware that later, from her own dream
Of elm allée or macadam, her own École
Des Rêves Joyeux, freezing but nourished

Past failure, by altitudes you sought
(And never reached), buttoned in Light,
Le Soleil, Sun, your darling child may yet

Smile back on you, having drawn from
The heart of the day's Devoirs her own
Cold nerve and poetry . . .

On the Day After

(in memory of E. M. .S.)

A dark amethyst light
A dark twilight in the morning
Falls on red clay and granite—

On petunia-white soft faces
Amethyst-hard shadows grow.

A storm is coming, one daughter says.
And one: My toothache aches all over me.

Death, a sunburst on the road,
Came yesterday. Now, twilight
At dawn and death at home,
The storm draws near. One daughter
Says of the night between, It's over.
And one says, No.

Soon trees knee-deep in snow
Will shadow amethyst bird tracks
And then your tracks

As they go, daughters not my daughters—
"Where will you go?"—

    "Out to assess the damage."

THE PINK MADONNA

The Red Pear Tree

Beside the red pear tree
And the ice-crusted pond, ready
To push off in broken shoes,
Antonio stands with his back to school.
He would not care if they told him
About genius, or how a barefoot
Freezing boy once pushed Samuel Johnson
In his chair across the London ice.
Which would he admire? The genius or
The skater raw and panting under
An ordinary mind and an extraordinary burden?
It is enough for him to skim a moment,
A rose-red-shirted boy springing
Away from the dark schoolroom and
Darker more forbidding home—to fly,
To be his own flame budding,
Skating in cracked black shoes
Beyond cold History and the red pear tree,
                              Free . . .

Here Lies

here lies the good child
who early on understood
what scholars said, and wild
to wear their laurels, fled
from home through weltering words
in the dark to find, instead
of a lost child's frail song,

weedy waves over deep woods
of green words risen in flood
where the orphan child stood
ankle- then knee-deep in blood
of knowledge drained and swilled

down by scholars drunk in the dark,
all dazed and reeling, their guild
undone by words netted then nailed
wrong into the dank wood of their world
and in the aged and oaken dark swirled

through what no good child could
honor at the end by calling "good"—

those poor greedy souls who should
at least have sewn a sail or emerald song
for the one who went wrong with words
having drunk from their tankard of dark,
Darkness, and too late understood
why it was, though they had sadly failed,

it was the child who bled

Two Views from the Sangre de Cristos

I

through the gap where the light
falls
in the V of the mountain's throat
the view   stand just here   the view
opens out a fine raw silk fan
a moth wing dusted with light
or a piece of bright lint
brushed up from a sunny condo rug
in the town   all dusty glitter
and tiny seen from here
as an infant's bead bracelet
or the ankle band of an eagle
overhead   holding all houses
all fans and fine feathers
together
and you too looking back
up   and   out   mute
a flake of light watching
egos rise in eyes large

each one as the entire town
seen from up here   always
with room for one more light-dazed
iris to seize baubles of ice
or jabots of light
from the long throats of women
swollen with mea culpas and cries
for wood fires near smoky births
among those moth wings
rising there to here—

II
stand back please   tell me   help me
seize for my own mind's eyes
this space fanned open   tell me
here or there in the dim far sparkling
which view is grander   before distance
closes and the light   the Light
                dries away our last hosannas

Only God Knows

God knows if it was the right thing to do.
Only God knows if what the seed foretold
Of this one flowering, this dark-veined
     opening, was true:

If it was wise for the man in pin- or prison-stripes
To go on climbing the stone stairs to Justice.

Only God knows or can imagine the skull
In the desert drying, or a rosy brain alive
In a stone cell praying for rain of a kind,
Something fluid with which to rinse away pain
Though suffering on, while the Just and the Unjust
Both try to decide if "it was the right thing to do."

Imagine the seed of the act before its bold
Blossoming—alone but fresh, rare, a-blush
With enterprise—No? Then climbing marble
Stairs, trying to hold erect and proud as though

Hearing inside that "it was indeed the only, the
   right thing to do."
Dreadful to be aware how worn-out by Justice
He is, how dire for us His weariness—dreadful
To wonder where truth lies when it grows free
Of the seed God knows, when only God knows
   If He is truly there . . .

Essence

what you are

wild currant leaves in a white china pitcher
in the wide light moment before twilight

what you are
when saffron scarves at the throats
of hills far away and white bones wait
where they say lions mate in the desert
        by moonlight

what we see you are
(in blue-striped white rough cotton and silver beads
from deserts far away   fades in a twilight once
clear as the foreheads of hills or beautiful women
near naked sands where moonlit lions play)

comes slowly forward   all the rest falls away

till what you are shines clear in our lamplight
as scent of wild currants in a white pitcher
or highlights   on the curved china like daylight
on the cheeks of unformed   promising girls

your gift   what you are
the pungent rough bouquet

Advice from a Spinster

"Let us love better."
            —*Emily Dickinson*

An old box-elder bug thinned down by cold
Crawls in red-blazoned shield close to the fire
And the dim red mate sprawled out to greet him.

We are at home tonight, generations
Grown coppery-red as the fox in the field
By firelight, but tired; trying so tired
To say what must be hotly said
In answer to the cold rage coming;

We watch the slow red insects flush
And fatten by our fire, exchanging shields.

Dear ones, guarded or not,
There's nothing left to do but love;
No way to prepare (as we brush ardent bugs away),
But face to blazing face across red fields of fire,
To swear we will obey our spinster friend
by loving better, if we can in time.

Nettles

here in the bare field you own
there are nettles under your hand
there is water somewhere below

it is hard work standing alone
not knowing how to begin
there are nettles under your hand

old weeds to clear away first
dry rage at growing alone
here in the field you must work

you are crying dying of thirst
determined to harvest alone
there is danger under your hand

it is hard work beginning again
though water lies somewhere below
to feed the green field you will win

never say never to love

Outcome

all Emily loves tonight is weather
and all that she trusts is stone

if Time were to bind old ways together
and mild days gently flesh out bone

might the lithe rose tree of her mind
slowly expose its radiant grain

to Creation's brown and calloused hand
that lays down love on rock through rain

might a light-veiled Emily then discover
on the bare moor of her naked soul

wild scents of hope like heather over
what it means to ripen and grow whole

knee-deep in promises sweet to gather
from rain-fathered gardens sweet to own

though now she loves only forbidding weather
and all she dares trust tonight is stone . . .

Mateo I

Mateo
wait

dreaming   slow
days like kind mothers
who gather
to splash water
over children in white porcelain tubs

when twilight
pale as olive leaves
leans
over a glitter of seeds

dream

you are fed once again
in a cool kitchen
ice from the old icebox
melting

bath water rushing
into the white tub   upstairs

dream you wait

for someone simple
and eloquent
as a kind mother
wearing amber beads

to lean down at twilight
        and gather you in

189

Mateo II

When they come running
　　What will you do?

　　Will you join them
　　　　and run, too,
　　Waving your fear, that poor flag?

Will you whine,
　　"I am orphaned.
　　I have slept with nine thin girls.
　　But I still don't know what love is"?
　　(Confession is good for the cadres.)

Or will you, crying and afraid,
　　Orphan that you are,
　　Say,
　　"I will stay till I find her.
　　I will stay."
　　Then stay
Till you can tell a mere flag from a banner?

Mateo III

Mateo, learn
to love the bare bone
on the plate in the sun

then love
the naked plate alone
a garland of fruit painted on

make of fasting a joy

till you burn with love
for sun on the bare plate's
blue plums sugared with light

and make of waiting a feast

as you dream
juicy flesh on the bone
sweet past imagining, then savor

love again   the rare taste
of a ripe plum on a real plate in the sun

"Je Réponderai"

—*Isak Dinesen*

Je Réponderai:

With a shotgun from the far green hills—that is one way,
Or when a prisoner or desert rat runs from the gun—
That's another. In a garden of tin cans shining, where
Espaliered trees and men with outstretched arms plead
Then begin to mutiny and someone screams, another . . .

Of course, the ways are numerous as storms, stunted minds
Or torn tents on desert sands where young men drill,
And a young woman sees the gun and the truth clearly,
Then cries out as though giving birth to the old child
            already dead beside her—

II

An answer, of course, the way she held that child, or the way
We hold the chewed-on core of an apple, the way we observe
Lost gardens, bleached cities, sandstorms, wars and starvation,
The way we see what we call Truth; tells not only who we are
And what stands we have taken here on the true desert's edge,

(Where it all began, lizards slid away and drums began to beat
As they will till the end, when we stop seeing or trying to see)
But yields other stark answers, like empty open arms raised
To surrender all but victory, when weapons are thrown away
And a lifetime, unaware it is ending once and for all of us,

    Cries out in yet another way   again   *193*
    "Je Réponderai" . . .

The pink Madonna

*The pink Madonna in Nicaragua or farther away tilts
her head in its straw hat with ribbons; her palms are
cupped open to hold gold-foil roses before an old altar
crowned with fire and floored with death. Where her
hands end, fear begins. Her face, painted ochre and
rose, gleams through the dust over broken stones, and
over fear's afterbirth, the live bloody flower in bloom.
From far away we stare at her, at Sorrow itself wearing
a torn, pink-ribboned straw hat like a halo; we touch
her wooden hand, still open to strangers, though
against the dark that prevails there and everywhere the
question is not of our trust in her, but who the pink
Madonna, created by and for Trust, can offer herself to
in a world so foreign and depleted beyond her
crumbling altar these sad days.*

History Lesson

a man
in a long black coat
and a broad black hat
emerges
through falling snow

behind him a road
a charcoal fence
a village lost in snow
stretch back and back

no morning bark or bell
only the man
a bar of narrow black
walking slow
through snow and silence
nears

snow fell all night
snow blurs the past we wake to
are you awake?

tell me, will a face
bright as snow in sun
when day comes clear
appear at last
below the low hat brim
to illumine us?

we must go back
and back
to welcome him

remember
how once the Hasidim prized joy
dressed all in black
and opposed themselves to suffering . . .

After the Siege of Leningrad

Akhmatova

wrote of a willow tree
in the snow
that was all

a young tree
alive still
among the ruins

so simple, so frail
grand, gay, and free
she wept

longing to lead
the way beyond despair
at last

through silvery green
unimprisoned light
that could bend

like her heroic line
and rise, a small willow
in the snow or heroine

an Akhmatova, free
to heal silence

her profile a coastline
eroded but strong beside a distant sea

Profile

Across the gully is an old woman with white crimped hair
like a soiled wig framing a Grecian profile and an olive-pit
eye. A stooped old woman wrapped in dun-colored wool,
her feet in thick leather-laced old boots, props herself to
rest by a fence post, then, slipping in mud, struggles slowly
down to join those on the other side of the gully who wait
for the day's passing event—a cart stacked with gray-faced
bodies, or a carload of crushed bread loaves perhaps.
Where is the old woman? Of what nationality is she?
Whose dire war does she share? What will happen next?

Remembering Srebrenica

If you cry, it is because you still hear
Isaiah's beloved lie, "All shall be well
and all shall be well and all manner of things
shall be well"   in snow passes
        where ice crystals were then
        and are still the only food . . .

And if you cry with pain over the terrible
faces of children and their grandmas dying,
let me say again: As you wait
in mountain snows of a long-ago war
for relief or death, for prisons to open
and broken flyers or farmers to mend
        and walk out carrying children
        who revived once too often
        and so became you, haunted still, wounded
still by rage over suffering seen again
through frozen spicules and red nets of tears
knowing it is time for tears to burn
        both far away and here
        though no longer with faith that
        "all shall be well and
            all manner of things shall be well" . . .

Crossing into Zaire

far away a ragged clay-colored soldier
hands the last one   a child   her mother's wide
broken straw hat and aims the child   alone   west
from the bridge toward a locust-brown countryside
where we watch her run   hobble rather   the last
creature   this poor scared one   to go from
the bridge into Zaire dead ahead lying bare
on and on   there nameless and roadless   to find
dazed by sun glare   somehow   the place her mother
among others struggling and falling   fell   herself
hatless down through sun   offscreen hard by
the bridge soldiers still shove others with bundles
back using rifle butts as the child   the last one
        to be released   a small agony
            lurches slowly forward
                directionless
far   far beyond us now   toward no known
        horizon   no horizon known to us

Child, I beg you to remember bells, the sound of bells over hoar frost, war, and brown morning fields. It will be a long time ago. You will be saying, "Goodnight, how early it grows late," and tears will toll in you for children crying in a steamy room where someone, a man, cried earlier. It is necessary not to forget ordinary bells— marriage bells, funeral bells, and solace, warnings, and tremors of joy over black ice (or over the child who ran sparkling across the frosty fields). I beg you, give to the perilous air that was already coming, clamorous and silvery, the sound of armor breaking into bells. Give to the child in you and to that child's sterling child the brown field you saved and held to hold out later—over the sound of crying, the sound of bells.

Black in the Snow as a Dancing Slipper

we know

after years of matching
thread to hem and blood to sunset,
letting out and letting down
muslin gardens for wayward daughters
to wander their burned-toast Autumns in—

after grief
black in the snow as a dancing slipper,
losses reeking of crêpe and cedar,
and passion hiding its tiny feathers
under Auntie's embroidery frame
while the Sunday joint cried out and bled—

after choices of mates and carving platters,
so many births in so many beds,
and spilled milk days by nursery fires,

we know
why genius through the green baize door
and intellect in the passage fled
from thorny gardens and long-stemmed chores—

free now of course, but too engaged
to sort old lavish trash of flowers
        for remnants of gold, a burning red

Be Valiant

Who says, "Be Valiant?"

Enough that we lean down to touch cold toes at dawn
Then rise to face one slow thing at a time—
A praying mantis gawky on a grape leaf
Or love's face dented dark by time, facing
The last star in the night window:

"Be sparing with your tears," they mean,
Officious with fear and unaware that
Souls like ours refuse even *kind* generals
For guides. Thank you. We'll find the way,

Stumbling on our own through arbors
Lavish with laughter or forbidden tears,
Where transparent wings of pain hide
On a grape of shade. We'll harvest

And preserve ripe fruit, sealed
With hungry care in clean Mason jars
Forever, and on our own, alone, wait

As the last star marches into pallor
And the beloved face fades—to try
And touch our toes again at dawn.
Who dares command us to be valiant?
Stumbling, stubborn, and afraid,
    we already are.

Barley's Map

Her mission: to meet herself walking,
To welcome herself in that hunched
        figure in the snow

Near a row of wild ducks on a floe
In the storm, motionless below the pines.

Her eyes blurred by snow crystals
Burning to behold what she will never be.

She walks far but cannot find one soul
        running wild—
Only a huddled woman scarved in air

Voluminous and dark. Snow falls
On wild ducks frozen there; snow falls

On water and on snow and her.

Juniper Reaches Out

Old Juniper Woman
reaches out to us, smiling.

She knows us as she knows young rivers,
deserts afire, hens cackling anger,
birth in the sand, prayers for rain,
the rank stain of yarrow, and arms
        kinder than stone.

Benign and smiling, she offers us
clouds, dried apples and cornmeal,
her silence in our language promising:

In time
you will be brave enough
to cross the panicky waves
of the dangerous river that now
        divides
desert from Desert, lover from Love . . .

THE PINK MADONNA

The Mesa We Climbed

The mesa we climbed has no twin

Just as no light on pine tree or snow,
No face lit by love has a twin.

Together we discovered
Landscapes and seasons to live in
And part of us knows now
Not how foreign they were,
But how it is to be foreign
Anywhere,

An alien stifled by silence,
Who must break out again
Into light unlike the sovereign
Light we climbed, must
Set out to find, neither
Escape route nor neighborhood—
But a calm level space,
A terrain like a green mesa top

Where a new language might arise
With or without pine tree or
Snowlight or house, saying

Now you are gone, how it is
To be alien anywhere—
Saying, Love,

The mesa we climbed has no twin.

Smike

"You were my home."
                —*Nicholas Nickleby*

you were my home
I live there still

the heart you gave
tells me to go
where live things grow
tells me to range
out far and change
and so I will
my guide your love
where life is strange
your love my hearth
on star or earth
your will my fire
and passionate
already late

dear blazing heart
it's time to start
to change and grow

though I must go
you are my home
I live there still
and always will
and always will

Rilke's Angels

You asked for red rocks and wild flowers once.

Instead
I would have tall Angels descend the air
Over your bowed head, their massive wings
          rustling light,
Light scooping sockets from which flight springs
And stiff feathers gleam when they fold down.
Motionless, eyes even with yours, I would have them offer
Gifts measureless as those you possess already.

And I would have you unbend in their presence
          remembering
What the master of their silence spoke
When you first bowed your head to mysteries
You felt approaching—poet and Angel—
          the flawed man
With his creation . . . before they turned
To spread their sculpted wings, and ascend the air
                              again.

I would have you recognize those angels bronzed by light
     where you stand
Awed, applauding in the throb of heights, his words:
"I don't know whether I am a falcon or a storm or a song."

                                                                              ~

More:
I wish for you what you desire most, with supple fortitude
                                      and power
In the shadow of wings where even genius falters—
Your own plain song, plain rocks, red rustling
                                    flowers.

Remembering N. in the Field

We can't see him for the clarity
of the morning where he bends
in a blue work-shirt to mend
the wire fence—the clarity

of an immense field framed by white
midges, white butterflies, sun
and time, as one sturdy man
blurred by tears and whorls of light

leans to his chore without a shadow—
fine bowed head and hand and mind
set in the shimmering heat to tend
a smudge of bright cornflower blue

all erased by noon, a splendor caught
between wire fence and white sky—a
blaze too dazzling and intense
to focus on and follow into the white-hot
	heart of Light

Pretend You Give Me Your Hand

pretend you give me your hand
pretend we go out

early
to hear the mourning doves
in the field

pretend you trust me
so much you believe

their clear voices
rinsing the bare field
in the early morning

cry
as I promise they will

Rejoice   Rejoice

old friend dear one
thin pancakes wait
in the copper pan
inside

Goodbye

the black pine
alone in the field
   before dawn
fathers
cone-shaped small
dark-shawled bodies
broken from night boughs

carved rosettes of dream
scurrying
home
over the cold field

before snow
fills the high nest
or day
soaks through dark wool

at dawn when
father rests

and all birds call as one

AGE WITHOUT MEDALS ❧

Age Without Medals

Age without medals, loyal friend,
Is *not* a field without sun.

It is where you come
To rest after the long run
    And the hard rehearsals
For the next opening, come
With amplitude and courage
Intact, though your voice
Rasps and in Act III you
    . . . hesitate . . . but

Draped in dawn silks
Love gave when it directed you,
Your defeats concealed,
It is time to make your entrance
Dressed in gold like a ripe pear—

Time, unadorned and grand beyond
Patronage, pretense or pride,
To play that "most demanding role,"
The luminous old woman you have become,
Victorious, bowing to the rest of us
From your proscenium of sun.

Under a Darkening Blue-Green Sky

From her door she watches
The man
In a frock coat
Place his shiny top hat neatly
On the small green iron table
   In the garden where they met.

Later he and the lady wrapped
In a blue silk stole
Lean across the carved iron table
To whisper, to shudder and console
   For as long as they are able

Under a darkening blue-green sky
Where Time will sleep and she will say
"This is defeat," as he passes a bundle
Made of daylight and kisses
   Across the green table.

In the raw garden I watch them eye
Twilight—edgy and eager, with folly
And restraint under a majestic sky,
While she removes her deep blue stole
And they touch, clasping old hands . . .

Red Shoes Dancing

To be old and to have joined others who are old
    In an Old People's home
Is perhaps the least distinguished stay
    Of a lifetime—certainly the loneliest.

To enter on that cozy finality is surely
    The oldest endeavor,
And perhaps the least resolute way
    To salute a lifetime shaking to its close . . .

God forgive those of us who rebel
    And resist in red shoes
By dancing wildly below a cold sky
    Amid loud claims on our own helpless children,

Till we join the others who are old
    In the drafty Old People's home—
Who drift now on the enclosing sky,

Loudly, open, each Self in red shoes
    Dancing alone
    From now on . . .

Late in the Day in the Snow

Once you were amiable, a trusting
Creature, blessed with gifts of wonder
And hope—a true adventuress,
Setting out from your bedroom
With its flowery walls, for the cold spaces
We all must cross. You know what I mean?
Do you? Would you say you had come far
Already? Time is in the waves beating
The Northern shore—you will understand
Their message sooner or later . . .
Perhaps out there you will choose

Between enlightenment and despair,
    Late in the day in the snow . . .

Like a Violet Star

Just below her on the floor
    Of the woods,
The violet-sparkling woods
Where she paused and stood alone
On her way into Old Age,
What was it she found, what was
    Understood?
Not how to go to ground like a fallen stone,
But how to rise up, a wild flower
Opening out in sun,
Where like a violet star
    She stood . . .

Those Modest Large Stones

They say the mountains are praying,
Kneeling there in the rain,
    Praying . . .

For surcease of storm, what else?
Their stone knees ache in the rain
But they kneel, as I said, devoted
Children of Time,
In full skirts of light, heavily
    Praying . . .

Heavily, heavily praying
To rise through flowering
Fields one small lifetime
Away, and go forth
Like settlers in full skirts
Of light draped with distance
Brought home. Of course
    They pray,

Those scared settlers on the plain
Where the storms follow,
And of course they grow heavy with Wonder
Which is all they are, after all,
Wonder, those modest large stones
    In the rain . . .

In Autumn Wigs

Here we translate landscapes
Into women in autumn wigs
Woven of bruised yellow leaves
And crisp shining reds

The women are young, with carefully
Loosened locks of hair
Combed into disarray to match

What they consider to be the truths
They will assert. Large, young, fresh,
Full-breasted and self-assured,

But the women, fools
Unaware of their folly, stand
Forth innocent as an Autumn

Arranging itself for stormy weather
To come, when landscapes will glow
And then tremble, as a dangerous
    New season is brought forth . . .

Live Rosy Flowers from the Rug

"I am the burden and the gift,"
The Old One murmurs,
Spilling tea on the rosy
Carpet from Kashmir
Late on a cloudy day
When her daughter stands
Nearby, the curtains
Are open to let Truth in,
And it is time to face
That Truth together

Then pick live rosy
    Flowers from the rug . . .

Outrage

We are moving slowly, but our outrage
Is swift, harsh, sullen
    And eager to crush opposition.

You ask if there is hope,
And I reply, No, none is known,
    There is no hope for the outcome.

There is no longer even a good outcome
To be desired, like a silver
    Dish full of ice to lift and press

To the face, the lips, the hot cheeks,
Nothing is provided
    As we move, slowly, slowly

Beyond counterattack, to loss—
Defeat the only ending
    At the end of our long rush
        . . . Backwards . . .

The Frivolous Old Lady

In time remaining

The old lady,
The frivolous old lady,
Tried to lay down the rules
After a lifetime
Of disclaiming them,
Or placing them
Under the chiffon scarves
At the back of the drawer

Where she sometimes
    Hid the real jewels . . .

Someone Wavers Her Way

At home
That old woman has tender moments
When she sorts gray river rocks or leans
To stroke her own face shining back
From river water. Much is revealed
To her—much is known already—
How the motion of water beckons
Her down, how, as happens in Life,
Someone wavers her way into Danger,
An iridescent gleam
    Of hope on her face . . .

Ready to Eat Wolves

They are preparing. They lean
Over foods to be served soon
And call out to each other,
Their words colliding
Above the counter and falling
On this side where the Old,
The silent Old, wait,
Deserving—what? Kind
Words and warm red sweaters
To be worn at the last?
All that their hearts desire.
Though now they lie on their beds.
Mysteries laid open
In small rooms,

Hungry and waiting,
    Ready to eat wolves . . .

Herons

Once
The Ladies,
Herons
On rosy
    Stick-thin
        Legs, posed

In shallow water,
Looking around,
Horizon to horizon,
At broad noon
    Where everything
        Was possible,

And nothing rose
In the way
Of the journey
They would undertake
    In their soiled
        Pink stockings

To the end
Of today's brown
World, the only world
They know they can rise in,
   So far, at least,
      The one sure thing,
         Rising . . .

AGE WITHOUT MEDALS

A Plain Angel

A mystery!

How one gives up space
Gradually,
    And how gradually,
A winged creation
Pretends
To rise through air,
Reassuring,
Undaunted
    And diaphanous
As any plain angel
    Soaring
        Towards the end . . .

Who Could Not Find Himself

The man
    Who could not find
        Himself
Went on searching
Of course, along the shoreline,
Till at day's sober end
He walked slowly home,
Three salt-white seashells
    In one hand,

A dark storm sky
    In the other . . .

What Any Seamstress Knows

Letting
    Down
Used Time

Letting
    Out
Raw Silk
    Seams
And sunset
    Borders
Radiant
    Still,
Neck
    To hem,
And then
    Unpinning
Joy
    In place,
As any
    Goddess
Knows
    Is the common
        End . . .

Known to Flower Courage

In a conical straw
    Garden hat
The old one leans down
To shove her trowel
    Into the lawn
Again (where all the flowers
Died in yesterday's freak storm)
Before another storm
    Comes in,
Determined at best
Against a warning pain,
To plant for harvest later
The tiny seed
Of the sparse-leaved
    Stubborn plant

Known
To Flower Courage . . .

Letter to Anna

My Dear Anna, Anna Mañana:

I believe you understand everything I say, every word I send across the gray board fence outside, as I look from the west window of this small room, where I prepare for my departure (one day soon, perhaps) . . .

Somehow from your own place nearby, between the high, old plank fence and the rubbled hills that criss-cross behind it, out where every sunset lights on both small and full-grown neighbors—the piñon trees rising from harsh slashes in shale-strewn earth, out where you "Keep Track," and falter, older and more care-worn, near the scrub trees scattered among rocks and fine-curled blond grasses nearby—growing wild, some only a few inches high, all twisted, and all sought out by wind, nevertheless . . .

This very day, under dark reefs of cloud, you (all of you) are in motion—stony earth, gold weeds and branches. Yes, here you are, near three gashes in the raw earth, where a gold slant of shale rises among all that follows, slicing strands of bare trees whose branches show dark among other pale or dark slashes you confront . . . nearby, watching you, while you, in charge of everything below, assert yourself, and so speak out. Yes, somehow, speak . . .

Tall and ragged against the sky, thrusting down other rusty evergreens' pointed tops and hoisted dark branches that impress and part gray and naked space, opening all the way down the black juniper trunks that rise through deep blue air and climb from gully and fence and crest, as you stare over low dark green forest growth and self-aware gold rocks (See this now along a churchlike ridgeline, remote and unstable, but designed, perhaps, to salve loss and so at last, let Light break through . . .

And as for you, Dear Anna Mañana, you are the tallest, most twisted, yet most attractive tree (in spite of some baldness, and the crookedness), with all your shape and distance asserting a strange, bold and as yet unreadable design . . .

Anna Dear, forgive both my intrusion, and my sudden awareness of your disorderly struggle to take over the entire hillside that angles up, as you also rise from a homesite rooted in strong rubble . . .

Yes, up to the wealth of sky you have earned—those blue fertile acres of air imprinted by small, bare, tangled branches, wind-torn and broken free here and there . . .

Well, I know I tend to be—extreme. But this landscape where we live, is itself extreme . . . Magical, wild and unfortunately for us, perhaps, stern, sad and demanding, too. Rooted out there, immobile in your rutted space, and signaling—we can't tell yet for sure—either wrecked hopes, or the ongoing

     Stubborn
        Resilience
           Of Joy . . .

And So Today

And so Today
The man in black
Leans on a sallow sky,

Crying out to us,
His timid flock,
To wake up boldly, yes,

And rise with wings
Stretched open wide
In rare comity,

With trust at last,
Flung out above
Our dangerous,

Our sad and powerful
Dark prey . . .

239

Our Leader . . . An Unholy War

Our Leader,
    Who peels the Truth
        With rosy skin,
            Clean from the core

240

To hand
    Around
        To hungry men
            Who ask for

Something
    More (or
        Less) before
            Setting out

Again
    To face
        The mindless war
            The Leader

Chose, trying
    To order
        Bravely or
            For the joy of it,

With Pride,
    Diving
        Down
            To aim at

And destroy,
    Legions
        Of Fear,
            Replaced

At last
    On our
        Innocent blue sky,
            Besmirched,

                Perhaps, Forever?

For Better or Worse

Not that noon darkened
And the creek overflowed,
Nor that after his death
She felt he had never loved her,
Not that her mind had altered
And betrayed her
For perhaps the tenth time
(Without her knowing it),

It was only that, later still, closer to noon,
When tinny bells rang out
And she started the washing again,
In the cold small room
Where shadows arched hands
And danced about her—yes,
Over that mournful morning,
While sudsy clouds danced too,

Filling her day with sorrow
For her troubles,
As she washed herself, alone
In the shadow her mind cast
On the death long years ago
That she still held close and mourned,
Certain at last
That she had lost him . . .

In the Late Light

To be captive
In an ordinary place
In the late Light

As birds wing across
The window outside,
To be captive

Here is painful
Beyond telling,
But to be free

Would be hazardous
In the late light,
On the gashed air

In the shadow of
wings colliding,
Perhaps colliding

Everywhere, as
Danger rips through
The ordinary place,

Concealed
By the falling
Light and things

Broken and closed
Down,
Plunging now

Through the late light

Into the end . . .

Beyond Honor

Though I am short I am the leader.

Here I retain my power (believe me),
So let them beware, those others,
Pale and wavering on the hard rock walk,
And shaken by fear. Let them beware
As power rises in my blue knotted veins,
From booted feet to unruly hair. My power
Fills me, I speak truly and responsibly
(If I speak at all) to warn those others, still
Puffing along through cold air, struggling
With their shakiness—their dim fear—while
I speak of strength and wholeness, even dare
Them to be strong and brave as a rare leader
Must be who touches the poorest others,

Short though I am, I, winged, speak
Beyond honor, responsibly,
In the dry air, with light on my blue veins
As I ply the hard rock walk, hearing

Praise for the noble Self in my veins,
Ready to speak out
To those ordinary others
Both cast down and wild

And like me, each one
    Craving power . . .

In the Mixing Bowl

See how late
Afternoon sunset
  Obscures her mind:

How even her hands
Grow heavy, as she
  Grows too confused

To know
If she is being
  Punished, or somehow

Glorified
By pain, all
  Self-stirring

In the mixing bowl
While she stands by,
  Stubborn, and darkly

Focused on
The rising danger
    She doesn't care

About, not really,
Not needing
    The kind of sweetness

That will lie
Heavy inside—
    A delicious burden

She must carry
Near
    Her hungry heart . . .

A Journal of Joys

It is a journal of joys that dressed
Slow days when asters bent on their stems
And cottonwoods moved in light winds,
And you were here.
Nothing else happened.

Oh the bliss! . . .

A Live Dream

You are no good at packing?
All right, take nothing, go naked
Even—it won't matter—won't
Change the way your lips tighten,
The way your blouse slides
      From your shoulders—
Or any other outcome. No adventure
Is described in any book
Or summary of a book tossed down
And soaked by the snows
      You prepare to plow
Through in your dreams. Oh
But you are fervent, fervent—
Be glad on waking that your dream

Is a live dream, with a shape
      And a trusting heart . . .

With Certainty and Praise

Here are the hours of defeat
    To memorize
And pass along, long days
To tear apart, fold open
And write notes on—notes
Complaining about all
    The losses,
The losses of Time and Place,
And even Self, in a fine black script,
Elegant on a long white sky
Like a white silk dress,
In praise of defeat
Tonight, when all the doors
Should stand open and
All the light should
Stream through,
And what is learned
Erase itself down
To the frayed white page,
The long day memorized,
Ready to be passed on,
And graded at last,
    With certainty and praise . . .

BIBLIOGRAPHY

Some poems from *The Travelling Out and Other Poems*
appeared in *Inscape* and *The Desert Review*

"The Travelling Out" appeared originally in *The New
Yorker*

The poems "Anita with White Lilacs," "Whisper for K"
(called "Whisper for a Daughter" here), and "Desert
Almanach" first appeared in *Poetry*

"When The People Are Avenues" first appeared in *Poetry*

"Dark By Dark Is Taken" first appeared in *The Lightning
Tree Journal*